P9-DBP-546

MARK TWAIN

Immortals of Literature

MARK TWAIN

By Monroe Stearns

Franklin Watts, Inc.
575 Lexington Avenue, New York 10022

TO
MICHAEL

FIRST PRINTING
Library of Congress Catalog Card Number: 65-13679

Printed in the United States of America

CONTENTS

FOREWORD

While George Bernard Shaw was waiting to meet Mark Twain in London in 1907, he told a reporter: "Mark Twain is by far the greatest American writer."

It was no idle comment from possibly the greatest British writer of his time and a man who had no small opinion of his own genius. Shaw went on to say: "I am speaking of him rather as a sociologist than as a humorist." Later he wrote Mark: "I am persuaded that the future historian of America will find your works as indispensable to him as a French historian finds the political tracts of Voltaire."

Now almost a century has passed since the close of the period of American life—roughly 1835–1870—which Mark Twain pictured as a poet rather than recorded as a historian. Shaw's judgment seems valid, for the best historian is the one who evokes the spirit of a bygone time and leaves the letter to the chronicler.

The works are, of course, fiction. Even when Mark Twain was recording his own experiences, as in *Life on the Mississippi* and *Roughing It,* he made the truth truer by arranging it into the pattern of a good story. The characters and the incidents of the books, therefore, can move beyond the confines of their bindings and speak across the years. They tell of a way of life even more than of themselves, revealing the essentials out of which their society was made.

In the American South and West, which Mark Twain took as his canvas, this was an agrarian society, scarcely contaminated by the complexities of industrialization. Now, the situation has been almost completely reversed. Consequently Mark Twain's creations are valuable for representing the simple elements necessary for the artistic construction of any other portrait of America. For though they are most certainly individuals, they are also types.

This is a major reason why Ernest Hemingway called Mark Twain the father of American fiction. Probably no significant American novelist since Mark Twain has failed to study the lessons of *Tom Sawyer* and *Huckleberry Finn.* Thomas Wolfe's Eliza Gant owes as much to Aunt Polly as Hemingway's Nick Adams or J. D. Salinger's Holden Caulfield owe to Tom and Huck. A list of the writers with a debt to Mark Twain would be endless.

Mark Twain is an important sociologist also because he was a humorist, not a satirist. He saw human beings as puny and impotent in relation to the grand scheme of the universe, but nonetheless triumphant in being able to accomplish anything at all. He applauded them as if they were trained seals tootling *Yankee Doodle* on a bugle, not well by any means, yet superbly in view of the difficulties involved. Thus he abstracted the enduring essence of the human condition. Had he been a satirist, he would have condemned his "damned human race" for failing to be the gods they ought to be. The substance of his works would have perished along with the particulars he was attacking.

Foreword

Mark Twain chose his characters and his incidents from the main currents of American society, not from the backwater pools and marshes. In contrast, the creations of his subtler contemporary, Henry James, are so complex as to baffle the casual reader. Their habitat is the drawing room, and the air they breathe is tainted with the exhalations of other indoorsy human beings. They particularize rather than generalize human nature. Though they reveal aspects of American society, they are too effete to have had many descendants. On the other hand, Mark Twain's characters and their progeny are the vigorous "picturesque peasantry," the lack of which the oversophisticated Henry James deplored in America.

As in the case of every other great author, much of Mark Twain's considerable literary output has not survived changing fashions. The inevitable progress of man's examination of himself and of his world has banished some of Mark Twain's titles from bedside tables to library shelves. And, of course, some of his work is clearly of inferior quality. Even Shakespeare has suffered similarly; only the specialist now appreciates, say, *Love's Labours Lost* or *Titus Andronicus*.

Fanatics have attacked Mark Twain's works because of the frequent appearance in them of the now outlawed term "nigger." During Mark's lifetime it was frequently used in the South to refer to a Negro slave, especially by uneducated and provincial people. It signified no particularly scornful intentions. The slaves referred to themselves by the term, often humorously. In using it, Mark Twain was simply reproducing the common speech of the South. He had great appreciation and respect for the Negro, and disapproved of the institution of slavery. As if to compensate in some way for its evil, he paid the expenses of a Negro, Charles W. Johnson, through the Yale Law School; and he ardently supported the cause of Frederick Douglass, a spokesman for the Negroes, in a matter of school integration.

Possibly the place Mark Twain still holds in the hearts of present-day readers is indicated in an anecdote recently told the present writer. An editor was visiting a famous contemporary author. As the editor was saying good night, he picked up a copy of *Huckleberry Finn* from the author's desk.

"I believe I'll take this upstairs to read in bed," said the editor.

"If you do," replied the author, "what will I have left to read?"

1

OUT OF THE CRADLE

The night sky of April 20, 1910, gleamed with a strange celestial body. Actually speeding through the heavens, it seemed motionless, like a gigantic flaring comma. All over the globe thousands of people came out of their houses to stare at it. Most of them believed its appearance meant that the even sentences of progress would be punctuated by some extraordinary event.

It was Halley's Comet, last seen almost seventy-five years before. It had shone in 1066, as the Normans prepared to conquer England; and in 1456, as the Turks were sweeping over Christian Europe; and, in all, twenty-nine times since man first recorded and predicted its visits to his shores of space. In those twenty centuries it had gathered around it a mass of superstitious lore, not the least part of which was the belief that it was connected with the birth or death of a person of world significance.

In Redding, Connecticut, a sick old man was murmuring about the puzzle of dual personality. Not long before the mysterious stranger appeared in the sky, he had remarked: "I came in with the comet, and I shall go out with the comet." A day later he died. Mourning began for the only writer of his time whose name was familiar in every civilized country of the world.

The man was Mark Twain.

So he had been known for the last forty years of his life. His real name was so rarely used, except in legal matters and among his oldest friends, that it was almost forgotten. The personality it identified had been submerged in that of the witty public speaker, the humorist, the creator of deathless characters in immortal stories.

He had come in two months before he was expected, as if to keep a date with the celestial visitor. For the comet had shone a fortnight before Jane Lampton Clemens gave birth to her sixth child and fourth son on November 30, 1835, in a rented two-room frame house. Its appearance was notable for the brilliance of the streaming tail. Later the boy would think of his birth in terms of Wordsworth's lines, "trailing clouds of glory do we come From God, who is our home." He would try desperately to find that home again.

Jane and her husband, John Marshall Clemens, named the puny infant Samuel (for his paternal grandfather) Langhorne (after an old friend, possibly a cousin). For at least the first two years of his life he barely survived in the "almost invisible little town of Florida," as Mark Twain was to refer to it, in the near-wilderness of backcountry Missouri.

The Clemens family had emigrated there from Kentucky by way of Tennessee. For ten years they had been on the move, searching for the promises the developing country to the west offered emigrants not blessed with an inheritance of rich lands east of the Alleghenies or of industries in New England. They had been disappointed, for either ill luck or a lack of foresight and judgment on the part of Mr. Clemens—he was generally called Marshall—had landed them just out of the best regions. Their fortunes dwindled, but their hopes remained strong. Finally the enthusiasm of Jane's brother-in-law John Quarles for the prospects of the brand-new village of Florida, Missouri, tempted them to pull up stakes once more and join him there.

At first they prospered from Marshall Clemens' storekeeping. The Salt River, which might have connected Florida with the commerce of the Mississippi, was thought to be navigable. The chance of sharing in the river trade had brought many a speculator to the village, which was struggling to stay alive just as desperately as the youngest Clemens, who had "increased the population by one per cent."

In the long run, Samuel fared better. Shortly the Salt River proved unfit for steamboats. Florida was long to remain a muddy, two-street village of a few log houses chinked with clay. After the bubble burst, Marshall Clemens' austere manner as proprietor of a club—as every village store then was—ceased to attract customers. He did, however, have some success in practicing his real profession of law, and became a county judge. He kept the title ever after.

Sorrow came to the family in the death of their fourth child, pretty nine-year-old Margaret, when Samuel was not yet four years old.

The loss of a child was not unusual then. The Clemenses' third child, Pleasants, had lived only a few months. Forty per cent of all children born alive died before reaching adolescence. Diseases now almost unknown in America claimed them. Medical care was primitive, and in isolated communities often could not be procured at all. But the Clemenses were uncommonly distressed at the death of any of their family. This latest one smashed their hopes in Florida. Marshall Clemens disposed of his properties there and moved out of the backwoods to Hannibal on the Mississippi, some thirty miles to the east.

The death of Margaret provoked the first recorded instance of Samuel's extremely sensitive, almost neurotic, personality. While his mother was watching the girl sleep fitfully in the last stages of her fever, Sam entered the bedroom. He was fast asleep. He walked to the bedside and plucked at the blanket. Jane Clemens was no less superstitious than any other provincial woman of her time. She recognized Sam's action as an omen of death, and when Margaret did die, she credited Sam with second sight.

During his childhood he often walked in his sleep, especially after an occurrence that had disturbed him emotionally. Throughout his life his sleep was racked with vivid, often fearful, dreams. He took them seriously, sometimes as prophetic. They made him tend to think of himself as more gifted than the ordinary run of mortals and not too different from the dreamers of the Bible: Jacob, Joseph, and his own namesake, Samuel.

After the move to Hannibal, "Little Sam," as his mother called him, began to be aware of his family and his surroundings. In the twelve years he lived and worked there, few aspects of this environment failed to leave an indelible imprint on his impressionable mind. These imprints made up much of the almost inexhaustible capital of personal experiences which he would transform into new creations.

The family then numbered seven: Orion, Pamela, Benjamin, Samuel, and Henry, the children; and Jane and John Marshall Clemens.

Orion, ten years older than Samuel, was a solemn boy, always with his nose in a book. The family pronounced his name with the accent on the first syllable. They are said to have thought Ori'on sounded Irish. Probably they just did not know any better.

Too much older than Sam to have much to do with Sam's childhood, Orion later had considerable influence on his younger brother's career. Intelligent—all the Clemens children were blessed with brains—he was an incurable dreamer, and too philosophical to see but one side of an issue. As a result, he became impractical, vacillating, feckless, and ineffectual. Mark Twain, who respected Orion's integrity, wrote of him that he was "always gentle, always melancholy, always trying to reform the world, always inventing something and losing a limb by a new kind of explosion. . . . Poor old chap!" Orion is gently satirized in Mark Twain's *The Gilded Age* as Washington Hawkins, a gullible but likable fool, and as Lafayette Hawkins in *Colonel Sellers as a Scientist*, an unsuccessful play Mark Twain wrote with William Dean Howells. He referred to it as "that play embodying Orion." Orion also appears under his own name in Mark Twain's autobiographical *Roughing It*. Orion's misfortunes, which ranged from unsuccessful journalism to unsuccessful chicken farming, plagued Mark Twain for fifty-odd years, but Mark never lost his love for his older brother or failed to help him out.

Pamela, born in 1827, was a quiet, calm, helpful girl with an appreciable musical talent, whose health was frail throughout her life. She married a prosperous merchant and moved to St. Louis, where Sam often visited her, her two children—Annie and his namesake Samuel —and their widowed mother, Jane Lampton Clemens, who frequently made her home there. Pamela is the Cousin Mary of *Tom Sawyer*.

Benjamin, who took care of young Sam, died in 1842 at the age of ten. Little is known of him except that he was sensitive and sweet and was a favorite of his parents.

His death greatly saddened the family. Orion remembered the occasion as one of the few times he saw his father and mother kiss each other, as if that embrace might somehow seal up again the rift in the family unity.

Jane Clemens led six-year-old Sam into the room where his brother's body lay. Weeping and moaning, she made him feel the dead boy's cheek. Later she tried to explain the tragedy to him.

Sam walked in his sleep again. He seems to have felt guilty about the death of Benjamin, as if in some unaccountable way he had betrayed his brother. In view of the fact that Samuel Clemens was many times to reproach himself for events beyond his control, Benjamin in his brief life may have had an influence upon him.

Henry, the youngest, was his mother's darling. Sam seems to have been deeply envious of the affection their mother gave Henry, and to have considered him a serious rival. Henry is the Sid of *Tom Sawyer,* but Mark Twain, in his *Autobiography,* emphasizes that "Henry was a very much finer and better boy than ever Sid was." As a boy, Sam must have despised Henry as a tattletale and as a good, truthful, obedient lad. Neither was above firing rocks and clods of earth at the other. Later they became close, and Sam felt protective toward Henry.

Far more important than his brothers and sister in the making of Mark Twain were his parents. Of the two, he more resembled his mother, who lived to the age of eighty-seven. She had been born in 1803 near Columbia, in Adair County, south-central Kentucky, to a farming family once of some affluence and reputation. The Lamptons claimed relationship to the Lambtons, Earls of Durham, in England. Some members of the family vainly pursued claims to the earldom, which controlled a large fortune derived from the coal mines it owned. The connection, if it truly existed, was so slight as to be ridiculous; but Jane Clemens and her relatives, particularly her cousin James Lampton, were proud of it. As the Clemens fortunes waned, she would remind herself and her children that they were of noble blood. Although Mark Twain did not take the subject seriously, he rather liked the idea of a nobleman in humble disguise and used it in several of his works.

Jane is said to have married Clemens to spite a lover too shy to propose. More probably, she married him because she disliked her new stepmother and because her own father's fortunes were at a low ebb. At that time, 1823, John Marshall Clemens, with an inheritance from his father, was better off than the Lamptons. At any rate, it was a hasty and a loveless marriage, and it brought Jane only disappointment.

She was a woman of spirit, however, and there is no record of her ever having complained of her lot. She once rescued a girl whose vicious father was chasing her with a whip, and gave the man such a gentle, persuasive, and nobly worded tongue-lashing that he apologized and swore she was the bravest woman he had ever seen. They later became friends. On another occasion she snatched a whip away from a cart driver who was abusing his horse, and made him promise never to beat an animal again.

Capable of overflowing love, she was intensely interested in everyone she met and in life itself. She could find the good in anyone and sympathize with his joys or woes. Stray cats instinctively found her door, and at one time she was keeping nineteen of them. If she felt she had to drown their kittens, she warmed the water first, and she could not endure seeing an animal caged, even a rat.

She was sharp and witty, though always speaking in a soft voice. When she was in her last year, Mark Twain asked her whether it was true that he was a sickly child. She said yes.

"I suppose that during all that time you were uneasy about me?" he asked.

"Yes, the whole time."

"Afraid I wouldn't live?"

"No—afraid you would."

Slender and small of body, she hated housework and loved fun and dancing, but she strictly observed the outward forms of her Presbyterian religion, without being truly religious. She was intrigued by every newfangled patent medicine and system of cure—and there were plenty in those days, mostly of no value whatever—and tried them out on herself, her children, and the neighbors.

She was the model for Aunt Polly in *Tom Sawyer*.

John Marshall Clemens was of an almost completely different personality. A man of keen intelligence and considerable learning, and proud of his distinguished English and Virginian ancestry, he felt himself an unclassed aristocrat. The small practical value his accomplishments had in the frontier regions where he was doomed to spend most of his life made him bitter and silent. He found escape in the impractical and the impossible, tinkering with plans for a perpetual motion machine and believing that an ideal society as outlined in Thomas Paine's *The Age of Reason,* which was his gospel, might be realized. He was a freethinker.

Cursed with bad luck mostly because of his uncompromising character and naïve trust in others, he felt his frustrations deeply. His own father had not been affectionate toward his children, and Marshall Clemens was not with his own, except Pamela. He rarely smiled, and he took no part in their activities. Always of poor health, he was crushed by the burdens of his family and his tangled business enterprises.

Once, however, Marshall Clemens had known prosperity. Soon after his marriage he and his bride made the second stop on their journey in quest of fortune—at Jamestown, Tennessee, then little more than a settlement, but already chosen as the seat of Fentress County. Here he built a house of such splendor—it merely had plastered walls and real glass windows—that the other settlers were dazzled. Mark Twain described it in *The Gilded Age* in a tone suggesting that the villagers considered the young Clemenses snobs. At that time, too, Marshall Clemens dressed like a gentleman landowner in a brass-buttoned, blue swallowtail coat. These possibly self-conscious marks of prestige nevertheless gained him the respect of the community, and he was chosen county commissioner, first clerk of the circuit court of the county, and acting attorney general.

On the strength of this acceptance and the increase of his law practice, Marshall bought approximately one hundred thousand acres of Fentress County land at about $500 for the lot. It looked good to him, though it proved to have almost worthless soil.

"Whatever befalls me now," he said, "my heirs are secure. I may not live to see these acres turn into silver and gold, but my children will."

For once he was right, but his heirs grew tired of waiting. In spite of his dying warning: "Cling to the land and wait; let nothing beguile it away from you," they disposed of it over the next forty years for what they could get. Then priceless coal deposits were found under it.

The phantom fortune the "Tennessee land" represented had an ironical effect on Samuel Clemens, illustrated by the use he made of it as a theme of *The Gilded Age*. John Marshall Clemens is the Squire Hawkins of that novel. A better picture of him is the character of Leicester Driscoll in *Pudd'nhead Wilson*.

In his *Autobiography*, Mark Twain wrote: "My mother had a good deal of trouble with me, but I think she enjoyed it." At the distance of many years he could see that his brother Henry's unfaltering goodness was monotonous and "a burden to her but for the relief and variety which I furnished in the other direction. I was a tonic. I was valuable to her." To his father, Sam was a reproach as soon as he emerged from his early cautiousness and reserve. "My father and I," Mark Twain wrote, "were always on the most distant terms when I was a boy—a sort of armed neutrality, so to speak."

Between the boy and his parents there was a basic love and family feeling, qualified by his sensing his austere father's disapproval and the injustice of his mother's punishing him for things he had not done. This lack of the outward signs of affection made the child sensitive in a way that children whose natural craving for love is easily gratified do not become. Little Sam had to look to other things to respond to him and to which he could respond. He found them first in nature, all the aspects of which stirred him, then in his contemporaries, and finally in his own experiences.

In the days of Sam's youth, the father was the absolute ruler of the little world each family represented. Generally wives were too uneducated and too inexperienced in the ways of the world for their opinions to have much influence. A child was to be seen but not heard; his existence was acknowledged, but his thoughts and feelings were of no consequence. The decree of the head of the household was final and was to be obeyed without question. He was the god of the world of the family, the visible symbol of the all-loving, all-providing, all-powerful God of the universe, in whom children were taught to put their trust.

When that symbol failed or proved counterfeit, as it did in the case of John Marshall Clemens, a child could not help feeling lost. As he struggled to find his way in the desert the world came to seem to him, he could think of the authority and its rules which he was supposed to obey only as hindrances to his own progress. The father-god figure took on the semblance of an enemy against which the child had to fight for survival. Spiritually he would be doomed to wander alone, searching for an adjustment to the world in which he had become an outcast, and a rebel against a meaningless authority—longing someday to find through his own success and through love a new authority of his own.

These were the circumstances that formed the basis of Sam Clemens' character. From such come geniuses, those beings whose exile from a world that has rejected them is so painful that they must create a new world in which they and others are welcome and at home.

2

A PARADISE FOR BOYS

When the Clemenses arrived in Hannibal, Missouri, in November, 1839, it was a village of some one thousand persons, squeezed between the Mississippi River and a thick forest. Twenty-five years old, it had a successful newspaper, several business enterprises, and a bookstore. Mark Twain called it "a poor shabby little village" when he transformed it into the St. Petersburg of *Tom Sawyer* and *Huckleberry Finn,* but that was more to express his own feelings about it than to state the facts. Hannibal grew steadily and speedily. Fourteen years later it had a population of about three thousand.

This population was largely made up of immigrants from the East like the Clemenses, but there were many Germans also. Much as the inhabitants wanted the opportunities of this newer land, they also wanted to keep the customs and standards of the older, more gracious, ways they had left behind. All had been victims of adversity, but they kept that dark and established new levels of society on the basis of what they had been, rather than of what they were. Mark Twain wrote of this aspect of the town:

. . . everybody was poor, but didn't know it. And there were grades of society—people of good family, people of unclassified family, people of no family. Everybody knew everybody, and nobody put on any visible airs; yet the class lines were quite clearly drawn and the familiar social life of each class was restricted to that class. It was a little democracy . . . yet you perceived that the aristocratic taint was there. It was there, and nobody found fault with the fact, or ever stopped to reflect that its presence was an inconsistency. I suppose that this state of things was mainly due to the circumstance that the town's population had come from slave states and still had the institution of slavery with them in their new home.

Slavery was an accepted institution in Missouri, and the slaveholders justified it by citing the Bible's several passages which seem to approve it. A slave was first a piece of animal property; second, a human being. At the least, his owner took as good care of him as was necessary for his efficient performance as a machine—much as a city man today would care for a Cadillac, or a farmer for an expensive reaper. Marshall Clemens once whipped his insubordinate, sullen house servant and slave, Jennie; but anyone who mistreated a slave was severely criticized and even ostracized. When a boy, Sam Clemens once saw an angry master throw a piece of iron slag at a fractious slave. It killed him. The good citizens of Hannibal considered the action justifiable, but thought it foolish and reprehensible.

Consideration for a slave's feelings was a minor matter. A slave trader was despised. If it was economically advisable, a family of slaves could be separated for sale to new owners in different localities. The Clemenses, for example, hired from a neighboring farmer a slave boy whose constant singing irritated the high-strung Samuel. When he complained of it to his mother, she explained that the boy sang to hide his grief; he had been sold away from his mother. Sam never forgot the lesson. In 1874 he wrote the pathetic "A True Story" about his sister-in-law's Negro servant, Auntie Cord, who was proud that, as a slave, she had fetched a price of $1,000, but who had never got over seeing each of her children sold away from her. Mary Jane Wilks, in *Huckleberry Finn,* is heartbroken over the separation of slave families due to the auction of her father's estate.

Jane Clemens' attitude toward the slave boy Sandy was perhaps more characteristic of the northern slave states than of those where the overseers of the vast cotton, tobacco, and sugar plantations worked the slaves like draft animals. For a slave to be sold "down the river" to the owner of one of these plantations was a dreadful fate; it seldom occurred except in the settling of an estate. The threat of such punishment was usually enough to quiet any troublesome slave. In *Pudd'nhead Wilson,* Mark Twain made it one of the binding themes of that novel. A slave could be set free by his master, but any attempt by another party to free him, or by the slave himself to run away, was a grave offense against the rights of a property owner.

The older Clemens children could remember the gruesome excitement of the capture and punishment of a runaway slave. Sam himself knew of the trial of three abolitionists who were caught helping five slaves escape from Missouri in 1841, for his father was on the jury that sentenced the Northerners to twelve years' imprisonment. Their crime was considered more serious than murder.

The effects of slavery were responsible for the adjective "sleepy," which Mark Twain also applied to the village. The only real excitement was the daily arrival of the mail packet from St. Louis, or of a more pretentious steamboat, in the months when the river was navigable. Hannibal supported two hog-slaughtering plants—Huck Finn's father sometimes slept among the hogs—a cigar factory, and a whisky distillery. The products of these manufactories, as well as wheat, hemp, and tobacco from the farms west of the village, were shipped from its wharves. Hence, Hannibal was an important river port for northern Missouri, and a transfer point for cargoes destined for the West.

The boats were the principal connection between the village and the rest of the world. They were its economic lifeline, its means of communication, its source of variety and entertainment. Mark Twain describes the arrival of one:

> *Presently a film of dark smoke appears above one of the remote "points"; instantly a Negro drayman, famous for his quick eye and prodigious voice, lifts up the cry, "S-t-e-a-m-boat a-comin'!" and the scene changes! The town drunkard stirs, the clerks wake up, a furious clatter of drays follows, every house and store pours out a human contribution, and all in a twinkling the dead town is alive and moving. Drays, carts, men, boys, all go hurrying from many quarters to a common center, the wharf. Assembled there, the people fasten their eyes upon the coming boat as upon a wonder they are seeing for the first time.*

The boats brought not only mail and trade, but also people from other walks of life than those found in Hannibal: traders and gamblers; revivalists; circuses and minstrel shows; phrenologists, palmists, and quack healers or peddlers of "miraculous" patent medicines; sometimes a senator or an aspiring politician appealing to his grassroots constituency. To the eyes of the isolated villagers, who regarded a trip of twenty miles from home as a real journey, these people had traveled and seen the world. They were wonders. To a boy, fascinated by their tawdry elegance and preposterous speech, they suggested the glamour that surely must lie beyond the limits of the dull little town.

Sam Clemens idled many a summer afternoon away on the shore of "the great Mississippi, the majestic, the magnificent Mississippi, rolling its mile-wide tide along, shining in the sun." It was the road away from unstimulating, repressive reality into the wide, wide world that beckoned the dreamer. For daydreams are the property and the comfort of the discontented. When the tension between dissatisfaction with the present and hope for the future becomes strong enough to impel the individual into action, then the dreams get realized.

The boy's dream was to be a steamboat pilot, guiding one of those splendid, gaudy floating palaces down the river of life, around each bend of which must lie the enchantment of a new and different scene. When he was nine years old, he stowed away on a river steamer, but he was soon discovered and put ashore.

A more immediately achieved escape from the tedium of daily life in Hannibal was the annual summer visit Sam made to the farm of his Aunt Patsy and Uncle John Quarles near Sam's birthplace in Florida. The Quarleses were richer than the Clemenses, and their home was warmer and more loving. Mark Twain pictured it in *Huckleberry Finn* (though he moved it to Arkansas) as the plantation of Tom Sawyer's Aunt Sally and Uncle Silas Phelps (the Quarleses).

There, with his young cousins, Sam was blissfully happy. The thrill of discovering the wonders of nature in the free life of the country made him think of it as "a heavenly place for a boy." So he called it when he was writing his impressionistic *Autobiography.* Then he remembered his delight in "the solemn twilight and mystery of the deep woods, the earthy smells . . . the rattling clatter of drops when the wind shook the trees . . . the blue clusters of wild grapes hanging among the foliage of the saplings and the taste of them and the smell.

"I know," he wrote, "how a prize watermelon looks when it is sunning its fat rotundity among pumpkin vines. . . . I know how a boy looks behind a yard-long slice of that melon, and I know how he feels. . . . I know the look of Uncle Dan'l's kitchen . . . and I can see the white and black children grouped on the hearth, with the firelights playing on their faces and the shadows flickering upon the walls . . . and I can feel again the creepy joy which quivered through me when the time for the ghost story of 'The Golden Arm' was reached . . . and how dismal the hoohooing of the owl and the wailing of the wolf sent mourning by the night wind."

Uncle Dan'l was one of John Quarles's thirty slaves. Mark Twain gave him immortality as Jim in *Huckleberry Finn* and *Tom Sawyer Abroad.* The story of "The Golden Arm" Mark Twain retold many times, and used it in his public readings. Uncle Dan'l was typical of the slaves in their leisure time, when they were gentle and kindly, and loved the company of their master's children who were as intellectually immature as the slaves themselves.

Then the Negroes would tell their fantastic stories of witches and witchcraft, magic and charms, weird gods and spirits and ghosts. Possibly some of the Quarles slaves had actually known the jungles and deserts of West Africa, from which they had been transported and where today the backcountry natives still observe the primitive rites of their animistic religion. At any rate, they were not more than a generation or two removed from that background of fearful superstition, of taboos, of the intervention of the hostile powers of nature into human affairs, and of ways to counteract or prevent it.

Instilling the minds of the children of the American South with this ancient, restrictive lore was the subtle revenge the slaves worked on their masters. To the mind of a receptive youngster like Sam, however, their tales and customs opened a rich world of fancy.

Back in Hannibal there was the prison house of church and school. Sundays were not days of literal rest, but days of churchgoing for all the respectable villagers and of Sunday School going for their young. Sunday was the one day of the week on which the old traditions of the East triumphed over the freer ways of the new West, where profanity, drinking, and gambling were the general custom during the other six days.

Sam went first to a Methodist Sunday School, where he had to learn and recite Bible verses. It is said that he won prize after prize for repeating the same verses about the foolish virgins (Matt. 25:1–13), and he pictures himself in *Tom Sawyer* as having a very sketchy knowledge of the Bible. In all probability, he learned many other verses. Mark Twain's works are full of allusions to biblical characters and events, and often reproduce biblical phrases and rhythms.

When Sam was older, he had to stay after Sunday School and listen to an interminable sermon. His mother had by then switched to the Presbyterian Church. The sermons proclaimed the existence of Heaven and Hell as actual places; they vividly described the bliss of the one and the tortures of the other, and uncompromisingly declared the difficult terms on which admission to Heaven was based. Thundering emphasis was placed on mortal guilt and the consciousness of sin, on individual actions rather than on general intentions. It was degenerate, negative Calvinism.

Much as Sam's attention wandered, he could not help getting, Sunday after Sunday, an ineradicable conception of the importance of conscience to salvation. He began early to have doubts about a physical heaven or hell, but his awareness of the factor of conscience, which seemed to him a kind of predestined guilt, troubled him throughout his life. He did, so his first cousin Tabitha ("Puss") Quarles reported, "a great deal more thinking than was good for him."

His first school was taught by a Mrs. Elizabeth Horr in her log house. Sam was enrolled at the age of four and a half and at a fee of twenty-five cents a week. Children of both sexes and many different ages sat at desks ranged around three sides of a room, and one class recited in the middle of it while the others presumably studied. The curriculum extended from the primer to the "Third Reader" (probably McGuffey's), and from the multiplication table to long division.

Mrs. Horr began each day with a Bible reading—on which she would comment—and an explanation of the rules of conduct. The latter was an immediate challenge to Little Sam's already strong disinclination to arbitrary authority along those lines. On his first day, he accepted the challenge, was warned, repeated the offense without the subtlety he later would learn, and was directed by Mrs. Horr to go outside and cut a switch for his chastisement.

He was unused to switches, though not to corporal punishment; his mother used her hand. But he had roamed enough in the woods to know the sting of a backlashing branchlet. He decided on a shaving from the barrelmaker's shop kept next door by Mrs. Horr's husband Benjamin.

The choice by no means satisfied his teacher. "Samuel Langhorne Clemens," she said, terrifying him, "I am ashamed of you. Jimmy Dunlap, go and bring a switch for Sammy." The more experienced Master Dunlap soon furnished an acceptable instrument of torture.

After that first school day Sam told his mother he had no use for education, did not wish to become a great man, fully intended to become an Indian or a pirate and scalp such unsympathetic women as Mrs. Horr or condemn them to walk the plank.

He could have seen Indians of the peaceful variety any day around Hannibal or Florida. But he had already heard his mother tell of how his great-great-grandfather William Montgomery had been murdered by Indians and how his daughter Jane had outrun one and how her brother had been killed by another, and his wife and children captured. Jane Lampton Clemens hated Indians.

Possibly Sam had heard of pirates in stories told him by the slaves or by his older brothers and sister. He could not then read, yet after he learned how, he could have found many swashbuckling romances of desperate deeds on the Spanish Main, in the cheap literature of the time which was usually sold by peddlers. The golden age of piracy was not far in the past, anyway.

He had small use then for more sophisticated reading matter. If he wanted facts, he got them from Henry Clemens, a voracious reader, or from Orion, who read what was considered elegant for a young gentleman to know. Sam was too much of a nonconformist to follow such a prescribed course of reading. His familiarity with the literature of piracy and brigandage, with lurid adaptations of the wilder medieval romances, and with the melodramatic popular novels of the time, however, made him a leader among his companions. It also provided him an escape from his confining environment.

At the beginning of one school day Mrs. Horr read and explained the biblical text: "Ask and ye shall receive."

During her commentary, Little Sam noticed the large piece of gingerbread Margaret Kooneman, the German baker's daughter, had brought for her lunch. Fervently he prayed that she would give him a piece, but she did not.

Depressed and despairing, he told his mother: "I don't believe in saying prayers, and I'm never going to do it again."

Mrs. Clemens told him firmly that it was a serious thing openly to deny faith. Then she comforted him, reassured him that school would soon be over and that then he could go to the Quarles farm again, and made him a pan of gingerbread all his own.

Thereafter he was skeptical of the power of religion to produce practical effects.

Pamela was delegated by their mother to hear the younger children's prayers every night, after Jane Clemens had learned that Sam could outwit her own efforts in that direction. He would say them willingly enough for Pamela, but as quickly as possible so that he could the sooner launch into a vividly embroidered account of his day's adventures.

These nightly fragments of autobiography scandalized the neighbors to whom they were reported. Strict adherence to the truth was thought a prime virtue by these unimaginative, perversely moral villagers. They complained to Jane Clemens.

"I discount him ninety per cent," she answered. "The rest is pure gold."

Miss Mary Ann Newcomb, who sometimes boarded with the Clemenses, assisted Mrs. Horr. Miss Newcomb was a dried-up old maid and no favorite with the pupils. They much preferred the other assistant, a Miss Torrey, and organized a rebellion against being taught by anyone but her. It came to nothing, and the insurgents were soundly switched. Later, Mark Twain confessed: "I owe a great deal to Mary Newcomb; she compelled me to learn to read." But the uninspired instruction in this female-dominated institution caused Sam frequently to complain to his mother that he "couldn't see any sense in staying indoors and listening to an old maid and a widow all day."

Staying indoors, indeed! Sam knew well that the outdoors offered a far more valuable education. To the imaginative boy there was always something to be explored, some new treasure to be found in the forest behind the village, on Holliday's Hill (the Cardiff Hill of *Tom Sawyer*) to the north of the town, or Lover's Leap, with its romantic Indian legend, to the south, or on Turtle or Glasscock's (now Pearl) Island in the middle of the Mississippi, or in McDowell's (McDougal's in *Tom Sawyer*) Cave, in which there was a fourteen-year-old girl's corpse preserved in alcohol, kept there by her father Dr. E. D. McDowell, the famous but eccentric St. Louis surgeon.

The "pale, sickly" child had survived his mother's dosings and "the long sequence of fevers, bilious spells, and convulsions" with which he was visited and which made him reticent and physically slow. By the time he was nine, Sam was a wiry, slightly undersized boy with sandy hair, blue eyes, and small, delicate hands. Possibly he was too active for his high-strung nerves, which still brought him wild dreams that caused him to talk and walk in his sleep. In *Tom Sawyer,* Sid learns one of Tom's secrets through hearing him talk in his sleep.

Sam had plenty of companions: John Briggs, his closest friend, some eighteen months younger than he, and the Joe Harper of *Tom Sawyer;* John Robards, who frequently won the school medal for amiability; Tom Nash, the postmaster's son; George Robards of the enviable head of hair, who died in a far-off place of a broken heart; Arch Fuqua, who could snap his big toe; Theodore Eddy, who could work his ears like a horse; John Meredith, who became a ruthless Confederate guerrilla in spite of his sweet nature when a boy; Sam and Will Bowen, who became riverboat pilots. There were many others.

Their leader, at least in Sam's eyes, was Tom Blankenship. He was about three years older than Sam, and was the son of one of the town's drunkards. (Jimmy Finn, the original of Huck's "pappy," was the other.) The Blankenships inhabited a shanty close to the Clemenses at one time. In his *Autobiography,* Mark Twain wrote of this original of Huckleberry Finn:

> *In* Huckleberry Finn *I have drawn Tom Blankenship exactly as he was. He was ignorant, unwashed, insufficiently fed; but he had as good a heart as ever any boy had. His liberties were totally unrestricted. He was the only really independent person—boy or man—in the community, and by consequence he was tranquilly and continuously happy and was envied by all the rest of us. We liked him; we enjoyed his society. And as his society was forbidden us by our parents the prohibition trebled and quadrupled its value, and therefore we sought and got more of his society than of any other boy's. . . .*

Tom Blankenship was Sam's idol. He represented the complete and successful rebel, the romantic child of nature who is free from, and therefore above, the petty, corrupting rules of so-called civilized society. Sam identified with him because Tom Blankenship was what Sam wished to be. Mark Twain named one of his two greatest characters Tom, and used it as the name of two other interesting outcasts: Tom Canty in *The Prince and the Pauper,* and Tom Driscoll in *Pudd'nhead Wilson.* The name is similar to his own. The inseparable loyalty between Tom Sawyer and Huck Finn is another indication that Mark Twain thought of himself and his childhood hero as one and the same person, distinguished only by their kind of knowledge—formal education on Tom's (Sam's) part and natural common sense on Huck's (Tom Blankenship's).

Tom Blankenship later became a justice of the peace in Montana, and a respected citizen.

The boys were into one scrape after another. Sam, who learned to swim late but then became an expert, several times came near to drowning. Once he dared one of his friends to make a surface dive into the river as he himself could do to perfection. The boy went down, but to the horror of the group, did not come up. Finally Sam dived after him and pulled his lifeless body to the surface from where it had got caught in some submerged barrel hoops.

Another time, Sam and Tom Nash went skating at night on the frozen river. When they were about a half mile from shore, they heard the ice crack and saw it split into swiftly moving floes. Leaping from one to another, they had almost reached solid ground when Tom Nash slipped and got drenched. The sudden chill after such heating exertion brought on a fever which left him stone-deaf and partially dumb. Such were common effects of the ill-cared-for diseases of the time; they account for the credibility given persons who disguised themselves as deaf-mutes.

Mark Twain used this common device in *Tom Sawyer, Detective* and in *Huckleberry Finn.* Another example is the pathetic story of Jim's little daughter in the latter book, not to mention the true life story of Helen Keller, whom Mark Twain knew, helped, and greatly admired. The incident also appears transformed in *The Mysterious Stranger.* Young Sam Clemens, and later Mark Twain, puzzled over why he was the one to be spared in this and similar catastrophes. His escape increased his feeling that he was something special, the bearer of a charmed life.

Another disastrous escapade was Sam's, John Briggs's, and Will Bowen's dislodging of a huge boulder on Holliday's Hill to see what mischief it would make as it rolled into a Sunday churchgoing crowd. In terror they watched it get out of control, go bounding down the slope, narrowly miss a Negro and his mule, and smash a cooper shop. They never tried rock-rolling again.

Or they would "borrow" a boat to go turtle-egg hunting on Turtle Island. Once they decided they needed to own a boat, and so merely "borrowed" some paint and brushes with which to disguise the loan. Tom Blankenship fitted it with a sail to save them the exertion of rowing.

McDowell's Cave, two miles south of Hannibal, was a never-ending source of excitement to them. They explored its three miles of passages again and again, running the delicious risk of getting lost among them, as Injun Joe, a town reprobate, once did, and had to live on bats until found. (They never located the exit described in *Tom Sawyer*, but it had been discovered by another "lost" explorer.)

Pirate treasure they were sure was buried in or near the cave. They dug for it many times, once coming close to finding real treasure of a less glittering kind—a rich cement mine.

There was scarcely a melon patch they did not raid or an orchard they did not plunder, having discovered the sweetness of forbidden fruit. On the more legal side of entertainment, they had plenty of picnics, river excursions, Fourth of July celebrations (which in those days were elaborate and spirited productions), camp meetings, religious revivals, and organizations like the Cadets of Temperance, which offered handsome uniforms and parades to their abstemious young members.

Sam joined one of these, but resigned because of lack

of the promised activity. He learned to smoke and to chew tobacco, as most youngsters did at an earlier age than they do now, but he probably did not taste alcohol until later. Throughout his life he was a constant smoker and by no means a teetotaler.

In spite of Mark Twain's insistence that Hannibal was dull, Little Sam saw his share of drama. In that near-frontier village there was still roughness and violence, only half suppressed by the civilizing influences of the better citizens.

A harmless old man named Smarr once rode into Hannibal from the country on his monthly spree. Drunk, he reeled down the street, yelling that a prosperous storekeeper named Owsley had swindled Smarr's friends. Owsley warned him that such abuse was insufferable and that if it continued, Smarr risked drastic punishment. Smarr would not be silenced. Owsley walked out of his store and shot Smarr twice. The old man was carried into another store, where he died in about half an hour.

Mark Twain used this incident, with elaborations, in *Huckleberry Finn* as the shooting of Old Boggs by Colonel Sherburn. There may have been an attempt at lynching Owsley; he was tried a year later and acquitted on the grounds of "just provocation." Boggs was the name of a Hannibal shoemaker.

Sam saw a young man en route to the California goldfields stabbed by a drunken comrade and "the red life gush from his breast." He happened along just in time to see two rowdy brothers, Dick and Ed Hyde, trying to kill their uncle. He and John Briggs saw a widow shoot dead another California emigrant who was drunkenly abusing her and her daughter. When he and Briggs and the Bowen boys were searching for a runaway slave who had drowned, they somehow loosened the body, which rose head foremost to scare the daylights out of them.

Of all these gruesome incidents the one which affected him the most occurred after he had played hooky from school to go on some escapade with John Briggs. It had kept him out till after dark. Afraid to go home, where he knew he would be spanked, he took refuge in his father's dark law office. Before he went to sleep, the moon rose. In its ghastly light he perceived a naked man on the floor, a gaping wound in his breast. The man, McFarland, had been stabbed that afternoon in a reopening of the old Hudson-McFarland feud which Sam, having been out of town, had not heard of. McFarland's body had been carried into Judge Clemens' office to await an inquest. Sam lit out of the window so fast that he carried the sash with him. He got his thrashing when he got home, but a worse punishment was the haunting of his sleep by visions of the murdered man.

Mark Twain reproduced the feud in *Huckleberry Finn,* changing the names to Shepherdson and Grangerford.

Another event that vexed his sensitive conscience and increased his inclination to blame himself was the death of a tramp in the Hannibal jail. Sam and his friends took pity on this dilapidated but somehow romantic character and passed him food and tobacco through the bars. Sam spent his own money to buy him matches, then a new invention, and expensive. Previously people used tinderboxes, the ancestors of today's lighters. The tramp used these newfangled devices carelessly, and burned down the jail and himself in it. His face at the bars of the flaming building haunted Sam. He blamed himself for having remotely caused the tragedy.

Nor was Sam's homelife without incident. Many of the pranks recorded in *Tom Sawyer* he actually perpetrated. He did give pain-killer, a kind of liniment, to the cat. He did take Henry's punishment for stealing sugar. He did sew on his shirt collar to hide his illicit swimming, and

Henry did tell on him. And he did persuade his friends to whitewash the fence for him, for he was physically lazy, especially when unattractive duties were concerned.

In time, he advanced from Mrs. Horr's school to Mr. William O. Cross's "good common school for boys and girls," and later to J. D. Dawson's, immortalized as Dobbins' in *Tom Sawyer.* There he continued to distinguish himself as a mischief-maker rather than as a scholar. He found the dull, parrot-learning methods of instruction so boring that during their progress he was forced to find diversions, such as racing a louse on his slate with Arch Fuqua.

He was, however, an excellent speller and often won the spelling bees which for years were a source of entertainment both in school and at private parties. He forfeited one prize deliberately by leaving the first *r* out of February so that Laura Hawkins could move above him.

There was a warm childhood romance between these two, for if Sam's mind was impressionable, so was his heart. Laura Hawkins he never forgot, and they met often during their lives. She lived opposite the Clemenses, and liked Sam because of his gaiety and gallantry. But she said of him that as a boy he was "commonplace," had a "drawling, appealing voice," and often played hooky. Mark Twain used her name in *The Gilded Age,* and her character as Becky Thatcher in *Tom Sawyer.*

Laura was faithful to him, but he had other sweethearts—Bettie Ormsley, and Artimisia Briggs, and Jennie Brady, and Mary Miller, who broke his heart for the first time, making him, he said later, "as miserable as even a grown man could be."

Such was Samuel Clemens' boyhood. From the point of view of Mark Twain's literary work, it was the most important and the dearest part of his life. He drew upon it again and again for the material out of which he created his greatest books. Even into those not based on this episode he introduced reminiscences of his youth either directly or as transformed by his imagination. No other major writer has used his childhood more fully. In his case the child was certainly father of the man.

The glorious time was to end all too soon. At the age of eleven, Samuel Clemens had to shift from his carefree boy's life into a man's responsibility.

3

OVER THE HILLS AND FAR AWAY

No more than in the past did the fortunes of John Marshall Clemens prosper in Hannibal. Although he maintained a law office, the fees he got were not enough to pay the rent on his house, let alone feed and clothe his family. Neither did his storekeeping thrive. Mrs. Clemens had to take boarders. The family was forced to sell its one slave.

Mr. Clemens made a trip into the Deep South and Tennessee to try to collect old debts and raise some money on the Tennessee land, but he came home empty-handed. When his wife reproached him, he replied with a hopeless expression: "I am not able to dig in the streets."

Nor was he able to suffer an employer's direction; he walked out on a job in a commission house when its proprietor found fault with him. His credit at the stores was cut off.

Then, as the effects of the Panic of 1837 wore off, his finances improved sufficiently for him to build a new house, buy a piano for Pamela, and invest—and lose—money in a silkworm-culture scheme. His legal business increased, and his efficiency as a justice of the peace earned him the townspeople's respect.

All too soon, however, he endorsed a note for William Beebe, a Hannibal merchant and the slave trader who had bought Jennie. To make the note good, Clemens lost his house and almost all his furniture. Pamela's piano was saved, and she now used it for the music lessons she gave to eke out the family income. Orion was sent to St. Louis to learn the printer's trade. The Clemenses moved in with Dr. Orville Grant's family over the village drugstore, and Jane Clemens cooked for the two families in exchange for rent.

When the clerkship of the Surrogate Court, a well-paid post, fell vacant, Marshall Clemens stood for election to it. The villagers sympathized with his bad luck, and doubtless would have chosen him. But he had to go to the next town, Palmyra, to attend to some legalities connected with the Beebe note. A sleet storm overtook him on his way home; he caught a chill and contracted pneumonia. On March 24, 1847, he died, saying good-bye to no one but Pamela.

Along with the rest of the family, Sam was grief-stricken. He was flooded with remorse for all the things he had done of which he knew his father had disapproved. Marshall Clemens had punished the boy twice—once for telling a lie that was not, as Mark Twain wrote, his maiden effort. He had never punished his other children.

Sam's mother led him to his father's bier. To comfort him, she said: "It's all right, Sammy. What's done is done, and it does not matter anymore. But here by the side of him, I want you to promise me to be a better boy. Promise not to break my heart."

Sammy promised, but that night he walked again in his sleep, terrifying his mother and his sister. They thought he was his father's ghost, for Sam had unconsciously wrapped himself in a sheet. The effect of grief and self-reproach on his nervous system had been increased by the shock of watching through a keyhole the postmortem performed on his father's wasted corpse. It was several nights before he slept soundly.

In exchange for his promise to "be a faithful and industrious man, and upright, like his father," Sam had demanded freedom from school. His mother agreed, but along with Henry he seems to have continued at Dawson's school for a while longer.

Every penny was needed to sustain what remained of the family. Mrs. Clemens rented a little cottage. Orion sent money from St. Louis; and Pamela, who had moved to Paris, about fifty miles away, to teach a music class, sent home what she could after paying board. Sam delivered papers for the Hannibal *Gazette*.

Probably about a year after his father's death, Sam was apprenticed to Joseph P. Ament, who had moved to Hannibal, bought the *Gazette*, and combined it with the *Missouri Courier*, which he had been publishing in Palmyra. A weekly, it appeared on Thursdays, and was the oldest Democratic paper in the state.

Sam was now an exile from his own home. He slept on a pallet on the printing-house floor and got his meals at the Ament house—in the kitchen with the old Negro cook and her daughter. It was stingy fare. Even after he had graduated to the family table, his servings of food were carefully measured by Ament's spinster sister Judith. Mark Twain remembered her and young Mrs. Ament with distaste. Sam was lonely, and felt insecure and uprooted.

He was supposed to get two suits of clothes a year, but he was given only one. The "other" was made up of Ament's old clothes, which were twice too big for the boy and made Sam feel as if he had on a circus tent.

As the new boy, he had to clean up, build fires, sort

type, clean the presses, wet down the paper, make paste, fold and deliver the papers, and do any other chore that came along. He learned to set type, and being a good speller, soon developed speed and accuracy. He could run the job press, and was in charge of circulation. Since the Mexican War was on, there was frequent opportunity for him to issue extras—one of his duties—that carried hot news from the front, just received over the newly installed telegraph line to Hannibal.

In spite of the hard terms of his apprenticeship, Sam gradually outgrew his loneliness and began to take pleasure in having a man's job among men. He also began to acquire the newspaperman's tolerant cynicism as he saw how facts were adjusted to suit the editorial policy of the paper or the requirements of the advertisers and the taste of the subscribers.

Ament was a short, unimaginative young man. He ran his paper primarily as a political organ. But he had the intelligence to see that Sam had qualities he could use. After a year, Sam had become his favorite, and he relied on the boy. Sam became subeditor of the *Courier*. He learned to write copy by having to fill out Ament's articles when they did not fit the layout, and he lent a light touch to the paper's otherwise stodgy pages. He may even have contributed some verses, richer in sentiment than in poetry, intended for the eye of one or another of his girl friends.

A provincial newspaper in those days depended for its success more on its editorials, its literary contributions, its letters from hometown folks who might be traveling than it did on actual news. It could not afford to send reporters to cover events at any distance, and it published only telegraphed dispatches or, when it could get them, copies of fuller coverage by more metropolitan journals. It picked up many items from its exchanges; hence, a story might appear in many papers throughout the country and even abroad, as Mark Twain's early efforts did. Naturally, it reported local events in tedious detail, usually subjectively. Sometimes it ran a crude woodcut by way of illustration. The type was blindingly small and the lines painfully close together, the only relief to the reader's eye being the array of typefaces. Advertisements were run on the front page, which looked like *The Times* of London now. Primitive as such newspapers seem by today's standards, they had an individuality that modern journals, with their syndicated news stories and features and columns, lack. They expressed one point of view, the editor's, and satisfied only one group, the subscribers.

Sam had two companions on the *Courier:* Wales McCormick, a devilish giant of an apprentice; and Pet McMurry, a journeyman printer, who was a handsome dandy. Both were older than Sam. At first they hazed him, but soon they took him in on their jokes and their mischief and their midnight raids on the Ament larder. Sam could take McCormick apart intellectually, and they had many hot arguments.

Sam would sing as he ran the job press. Sometimes he would set up and run off on silk a popular poem of the day, as a present for one of his girls. He was usually through work by midafternoon, and so had time for reunions with his old gang. And he began to go to parties, where he was popular with the girls, in spite of the tricks he played on them. His favorite was still Laura Hawkins, the only one with whom he would skate arm in arm on the river or go flower-picking in the summer meadows.

If he had any ambitions at this time, they changed with the weather. One day he wanted to be a journeyman printer like Pet McMurry; another, he yearned to be end man in a minstrel show or a clown in the circus or a hypnotist. He even thought of becoming a preacher, but only because he imagined that a preacher's soul would inevitably be saved. Then came what he later considered an important turning point in his life.

As he was walking from the printshop to his mother's cottage, he picked up a windblown page from a book about Joan of Arc that told of her persecution in prison. It captured his imagination. Henry—or possibly his mother, though Jane Clemens read little besides the Bible—told him that Joan was a real person.

Sam had never heard of her before. Now he resolved to broaden the limited scope of his reading and learn all he could about Joan and her times. He developed a devotion to history and an appetite for knowledge in general. With John Briggs he got a German shoemaker to teach them German, and he tried to learn Latin. He even read the Bible through. From then on, he never lost his serious interest in the printed word. Joan of Arc's story introduced him to bigotry, tyranny, and oppression, and instilled in him a lifelong hatred of them and of rulers who caused them.

In the summer of 1850, Orion returned to Hannibal and started a newspaper he called the *Western Union,* using the press and the type he had bought in St. Louis out of his savings. He later changed its name to the *Journal,* and still later made it the *Hannibal Daily Journal.* It was a Whig paper. When Sam's two-year apprenticeship to Ament was over, Orion persuaded his brother to come to work for him. He also employed Henry.

Orion had hoped to be a lawyer and in St. Louis had read law in the office of Edward Bates. He had never wanted to be a printer or a newspaperman. He thought those occupations beneath him and accepted them in a self-torturing way as punishments somehow good for his soul. The family's need for money thwarted Orion's legal ambitions, and his landlady squelched his other desire, to be an orator, by forbidding him to practice in his room. He had no talent in that direction, anyway. Always impractical—the failure of his father's store was partially due to Orion's mismanagement—he was now a tall, handsome, serious young man with prematurely gray hair. His studious inclinations brought him few friends who might have tempered his bookish ideas with practical experience; and his desire for approval, which made him change his opinions to suit those of his last companion, brought him no steady friends. Already, at the age of twenty-five, he was branded with the repressions of failure.

Sam was quick to perceive these scars. Although Orion found his brother well trained and a better worker than Henry, Sam grumbled. He never had much use for masculine authority unless he fully respected the person wielding it. To him Orion, now the titular head of the family, was not even the equal of their father, for whom Sam's respect was qualified in that he thought his father had let them all down. Furthermore, Orion showed small enthusiasm for his new enterprises. He was unable ever to pay Sam the $3.50 a week salary he had promised.

Unlike Orion, who was an other-cheek-turning doormat, Sam was a rebel, and a constructive one. Orion was frequently absent from the offices on some unproductive mission or other, probably to orate for temperance and against profanity. (In St. Louis his colleagues had nicknamed him "Parson Snivel.") In his capacity as assistant editor, Sam took advantage of these excursions of Orion's by seeking to enliven the *Journal*.

The items he contributed are the earliest remaining literary efforts of the person who was to become one of the world's best-known authors. They are crudely executed and childish, but they contain the same impish, irreverent mockery of stupidity, gullibility, hypocrisy, and pretentiousness that marks his later work. Even at this early age, Sam Clemens could detect the incongruities in human nature that are the basis of humor. And his agile mind could quickly combine unrelated elements into a connection that surprisingly makes sense—a connection which is the basis of wit.

For example, he inserted a notice of the marriage of a Mr. H. Hoe to a Miss Ann Handle, and followed it with two stanzas:

How useless an Handle without any Hoe,
And useless a hoe without any handle;
No better a winter without any snow,
Or a candlestick minus a candle.

But here, joined in one, the Handle and Hoe
With life's rugged journey, smooth over,
And each prove a helper in this world below,
Till death shall hoe both to another.

Items like this increased the circulation of the *Journal.* It was the kind of crude punning, simpleminded humor, and obvious sentimentality ("life's rugged journey," "till death shall . . .") that pleased provincial readers in an unsophisticated community. They also loved stories about the discomfiture of a prig, a dandy, or a show-off—any exaggeration of conventional behavior or departure from it.

Sam Clemens knew this from experience. When the only boy in Hannibal to go to an eastern university—in this case, Yale—returned to strut the dusty streets in his campus clothes, it was Sam who dressed up a derelict Negro in an exact copy of the outfit and paid him to mince behind the college boy.

When the editor of the rival *Messenger,* one J. T. Hinton, a new bachelor in Hannibal, published an editorial about the danger of dogs running loose in the town, Sam ridiculed it, and drew an ill-tempered reply. Sam did not answer; perhaps Orion had returned and put an end to the rivalry. Soon it became common gossip in Hannibal that Hinton had been jilted, had declared his intention of suicide, then lost his nerve. Sam closed in.

The *Journal* for September 16, 1852, ran a crude woodcut, probably drawn by Sam himself since its style resembles his inept sketches. It depicted a dogheaded man with a walking stick, carrying a lantern, and equipped with a whisky bottle, wading into a river. Beneath it was an explanation:

> 'LOCAL' . . . *contemplates Suicide. His 'pocket pistol' (i.e. the* bottle) *failing in the patriotic work of ridding the country of a nuisance, he resolves to 'extinguish his chunk' by feeding his carcass to the fishes of Bear Creek, while friend and foe are wrapt in sleep. Fearing, however, that he may get out of his depth, he* sounds the stream with his walking-stick.
>
> *The artist has . . . caught the gentleman's countenance as correctly as the thing could have been done with the real* dog-*gerytype apparatus. Ain't he pretty? and don't he step along through the mud with an air? 'Peace to his re-manes.'*

Not exactly a subtle riposte, but to the villagers a masterpiece. The atrocious pun on daguerreotype, the bad grammar, and the vulgar vocabulary were what they doted on. The *Journal*'s circulation again increased.

After Hinton's violent reply to the "puppy" who had embarrassed him, Orion put an end to the farce with a characteristically pious editorial.

The circulation increased even more after the *Journal*

published, on May 6, 1853, a sentimental effusion with the provocative title, "Love Concealed; To Miss Katie of H——l." The next day's issue carried a letter signed "Grumbler," protesting that the abbreviation in the dedicatory line signified Hell, no compliment to Miss Katie, and a word never used in genteel, family-type literature. Grumbler's style is suspiciously like Sam's. At any rate, Sam replied that "H——l" really signified Hannibal. Again the battle was on. Sam had doubtless invented the whole thing. Mark Twain used the joke twice in his writings.

Among many other contributions to the *Journal,* Sam wrote a column of feebly witty comment on local happenings, and four feature stories under his first pen name, W. Epaminondas Adrastus Blab. The last of these contains a germ of what, with Mark Twain, would grow into polished humor: "The first Blab lived in Adam's time . . . but Adam was no more respectable than Blab—he never had a mother! At least people said so, and folks of that character don't stand very high nowadays."

In rebellion first against the authority of the mean Joseph Ament and then of Orion with his "slow stupid way," as Mark Twain described it, Sam was finding himself. His success in writing was showing him a way out of the emptiness of his life into acceptance by the world, and it was his own way as an individual.

The first indication of true recognition came with the acceptance of a story by *The Carpet-Bag,* a Boston comic weekly. This was "The Dandy Frightening the Squatter, written for The Carpet-Bag by S. L. C." It is simply an anecdote, and by no means an original invention of the author's. Sam merely made the scene Hannibal and retold the story in a direct, unadorned way. It is typical of the humor of the time: an elaborately dressed young man wants to impress the ladies on a riverboat and truculently threatens a brawny woodman on the wharf, who promptly knocks him into the river.

By this time the paper was not making any money, thanks to Orion's mismanagement. The Clemenses were getting scarcely enough to eat and had to take boarders again. Pamela married and moved to St. Louis. Sam got itching feet. When he asked the bedeviled Orion for money to buy a shotgun and got only an angry lecture on extravagance, Sam had had enough. He told his mother he was just going to St. Louis, where he could find work and send money home, but he had other intentions.

Jane Clemens sadly packed his meager things and prepared to say good-bye to her most difficult child. She held out a little Testament to him.

"I want you to take hold of the other end of this, Sam," she said, "and repeat after me these words: 'I do solemnly swear that I will not throw a card or drink a drop of liquor while I am gone'."

Sam swore, and he kept the oath to the letter—that is, during that one trip.

At the age of seventeen, the exile became a wanderer.

That night Sam's knees may have been a bit shaky, and his eyes a little misty, as the boat for St. Louis pulled away from the Hannibal wharf. It was the first time he had been away from home, the first time he was to be really alone.

He remembered the agony of desolation he had felt years before, when his mother and her other children had gone to the Quarles farm, leaving Judge Clemens to bring Sam the next morning. His absentminded father had ridden off while the boy was still asleep. Not till dusk did his young uncle return for Sam, who had spent the long, lonely day coaxing meal to run out of a hole in its sack, and was hungry and crying.

Now he believed that Orion, who in a sense had taken the place of their father, hated him. He was running away from the petty tyranny of these two failures, determined to become his own authority as soon as possible. Perhaps he took stock of the ammunition he had available for his combat against the desert of life that stretched ahead.

In his puny childhood he had found that the use of his intelligence could make up for what he was physically unable to achieve. There was one weapon. Jane Clemens, harassed by trying to make do in spite of poverty and disappointment, had turned her sharp tongue on him many times when his rebellious mischief added one more worry to her store than she could bear. Unconsciously she had stimulated him to reply in kind, and she had been generous enough to admire and respect his courage. He had learned to hold his own with his older fellow workers and even to turn the tables on them. He had proved that he was an efficient journeyman printer and that he could be as good an editor as Ament or Orion, if not a better one. And he had been published!

This little arsenal gave him a veneer of confidence. Yet he must have suspected that its arms had been tested only against pretty weak defenses. Perhaps they were not tempered steel, but brittle cast iron, effective in tiny Hannibal but ludicrous in St. Louis, the metropolis of the middle Mississippi—or in the wide, wide world beyond, to which his thoughts were truly turning.

Two pictures taken during his years on the Hannibal papers are a clue to Sam's personality then. The first, made when he was fifteen, shows an adolescent whose aggressive posture is betrayed by a soft and subtle smile. He is hiding his doubts as to his identity by overconfidently pointing at an enormous belt buckle bearing his name. The second shows a sensitive youth of seventeen, his intelligence marked by a broad forehead and widely spaced eyes, his tremulously insecure expression framed by strong facial contours and punctuated by a firmly determined chin. By this time, Sam's sandy hair had turned to auburn, and his eyes had acquired a greenish tint. He had reached his final height of five feet ten.

In St. Louis he found a job in the composing room of the *Evening News*. He lived with Pamela, now Mrs. William A. Moffett. Then after about two months he was either discharged or quit. He had nevertheless earned enough to continue his wanderings.

He sewed a ten-dollar bill inside his coat lining and, with the rest of his wages in his pocket, set out for New York to see the Crystal Palace, where America's first World's Fair was in progress. After five wretched days of traveling by railroad and boat he arrived on August 24, 1853.

That night he wrote his mother about his adventures, knowing full well that the letter would be printed in the *Journal*. It was, and all Hannibal thrilled vicariously to the wonders described by its native son who now "had traveled and seen the world." He had already visited the Crystal Palace and had seen two "wild men" of Borneo.

This promising letter was the first of many he would write about his later travels. One of its sentences foreshadows their sharp and witty observation: "I reckon I had better black my face, for in these Eastern States niggers are considerably better than white people." Fourteen years later, in the letters he would send back about his voyage to Europe and the Holy Land, he showed the same provincial wonderment at the customs of other regions, judging them on terms of his own limited experience.

Within a week of his arrival in New York, Sam had got a job in John A. Gray's book- and job-printing office at 97 Cliff Street, in the printing and newspaper district of old New York. Next door was Harper's, which would later publish Mark Twain's books. He boarded about a mile away on Duane Street, near the Hudson River. From the fifth-story windows where he worked he could marvel at the harbor and its "forest of masts with all sorts of flags flying."

In his free time he explored million-footed Manhattan, amazed at its crowds, astonished by its displays. His evenings he spent at one or the other of the printers' two free libraries. "If books are not good company," he wrote his mother, "where will I find it?" He was continually gratifying his desire for curious facts and useful information. He was learning to disguise his bewilderment at strange things with a mask of humorous and unconventional comment. He was acquiring a style, not unlike Jonathan Swift's reporting of Gulliver's travels. But he was not yet aware of mankind, only of things and of the easy generalizations about life that he found in books.

Like many another stranger in New York before and since, he complained that he had no one to talk to. And he hated the food. So, after having seen the sights and been to the theater, he moved on to Philadelphia toward the end of October. There he found work on the *Inquirer*. He liked the city better than New York, possibly because of its superabundance of monuments connected with American history and with Benjamin Franklin, the patron saint of American printers and journalists. Sam rather fancied himself another Franklin, who at the same age had left his brother's printshop and journeyed forth to become a citizen of the world.

After two months he was homesick. Winter was coming on, and Christmas. But the Clemenses had moved from

Hannibal to Muscatine, Iowa, where Orion had bought himself another newspaper. So Sam stuck out his travels for another six months, visiting Washington, then returning to Philadelphia and New York. Late in the summer of 1854, he boarded a train for St. Louis, sat up in it for three days and nights, then slept through the next thirty-six hours on the boat up the Mississippi to Muscatine.

He arrived late at night and spent the hours till morning in the hotel, memorizing outstanding events in the reigns of the English kings. He walked in unexpected on the family at breakfast and pretended to hold them up with a gun. Jane Clemens screamed.

"You wouldn't buy me one," Sam said to Orion, "so I got one and intend to use it—in self-defense."

Then he kissed his mother, sobbing with relief at being home again and in her arms.

Orion urged him to stay and work on the Muscatine *Journal,* in which Sam's travel letters from Philadelphia and Washington had been printed. Sam replied that he could not afford the luxury. He returned to his former job of typesetting in St. Louis.

There he could earn some badly needed money, and be near his sister. Money was becoming a driving force in his life. Financial self-sufficiency, he thought, was the quickest way to independence. He did not see that in spite of the confidence he had gained by supporting himself during his more than a year of travels, he was not yet independent of family and old friends.

Over twenty years later, Sam wrote to Frank E. Burrough, with whom he roomed in the house of a family from Hannibal, that Burrough was correct in describing him then as "a callow fool, a self-sufficient ass . . . imagining that he is remodeling the world and is entirely capable of doing it right."

That winter Orion married a family friend, Mary

("Mollie") Stotts, of Keokuk, Iowa. He was so absent-minded that on the morning after the wedding he got on the stagecoach for Muscatine, completely forgetting his bride, whom he left standing on the sidewalk. Mollie did not like Muscatine, and so Orion sold his paper and moved with Mollie and Henry to Keokuk, where he opened the Ben Franklin Book and Job-Printing Office. Jane Clemens went to live with Pamela. In the summer of 1855, Sam joined his two brothers in the business for a salary of $5.00 a week and board.

He stayed for a year and a half, apparently enjoying society in Keokuk and being a steady single man at the young ladies' entertainments. The girls liked him for his jokes and gay heart, but he did not go beyond mere friendship with any of them. At night he read a good deal, lying in bed and smoking an effort-saving water pipe until a late hour. He would even get one of his friends to light the pipe for him when it went out.

Frank Burrough had introduced him to the novels of Thackeray, Dickens, and Scott. Sam, however, never cared much for novels. He found Scott hard going. He could find nothing funny in Dickens' *Pickwick Papers*, and said he himself could write a funnier book. But he greatly admired *A Tale of Two Cities*, after he had read it later. His favorite reading remained history, but during his travels he had become familiar with the liberal thinking of Thomas Paine, which may have been responsible for Burrough's description of Sam as a reformer.

The book which had the most immediate influence upon him was Herndon and Gibbon's *Exploration of the Valley of the Amazon*, which had been published in 1853. It held forth visions of the fortune to be gained from cocoa in Brazil, and it set Sam's feet itching to wander again. Anything to get away from routine and stupid management, and into the big money and independence.

As might have been expected, Orion was not making a success of the printing office. Rather than try to pay Sam wages, Orion made him a partner. But he could barely make a living, for the business showed scant profits. Sam was dissatisfied. The account of Lieutenant Herndon's travels tempted him.

One squally November day in 1856, a fifty-dollar bill came toward him on the wind in a Keokuk street. Sam grabbed it. He advertised his find, but no one claimed it. Sam figured he had a foundation for the capital he needed to go to Brazil. Luck had provided him with a turning point as significant as the wind-borne page of Joan of Arc's story.

At once he went to St. Louis to say good-bye to his mother. While there, he thought up a plan to increase his funds, and returned to Keokuk to see whether the literary *Saturday Post* would buy travel letters from him while he was in South America. The editor agreed to pay him $5.00 a letter.

Then, by way of Quincy, Chicago, Indianapolis, and Cincinnati, he was off to New Orleans to pick up a boat for the Amazon. In Cincinnati he worked for four months as a printer for Wrightson & Company while waiting for the river to be free enough of ice for the journey southward. From Cincinnati he wrote his first letter to the Keokuk *Post*, describing his wanderings so far. It was signed Thomas Jefferson Snodgrass, the last name having been borrowed from *Pickwick Papers*.

When American correspondents, especially humorous ones, used a pen name, they were following a custom that went back to the early British journalists of the eighteenth century. Then a *nom de plume*, however transparent, protected the owner from libel actions and other forms of revenge. In America, where freedom of expression was constitutionally guaranteed, a pseudonym protected an author from the charge of illiteracy in an age when correct usage, correct spelling, and a refined vocabulary were so much the marks of false gentility that they were burlesqued by the comic writers. This was the broad humor that made the fame of Artemus Ward, Petroleum V. Nasby, Orpheus C. Kerr, Josh Billings, and Mr. Dooley—all pen names. The effect was to make the reader feel proud of his refinement, and superior to the barbarisms of the supposedly provincial writer. It was merely a form of the ancient gags about the hick in the big town.

Snodgrass began his first letter:

> *You know arter going down there to St. Louis, and seein' so many wonderful things, I wanted to see more—so I took a notion to go a travelin', so as to see the world, and then write a book about it—a kind o' daily journal like—and have all in gold on the back of it 'Snodgrass' Dierrea' or somethin' of that kind, like other authors that visits forren parts.*

A little of this goes a long way. Even in the 1850's the Snodgrass prose was an exaggeration of illiteracy and dialect, part of the "tall tale" that is the essence of American humor.

As usual, Sam stayed in a cheap boarding house with dull fellow lodgers, except for a Scot. This Macfarlane "had two or three dozen weighty books—histories, philosophies, and scientific works" and loved to talk about them. His own philosophy anticipated Darwin's theory of evolution, and he expounded it in terms of the Calvinistic doctrine common to Scots. All life on the earth, Macfarlane claimed, started from one microscopic germ and developed from it in a progressively ascending scale until it reached perfection in man. Then the scheme broke down. Man was sinful and used his intellect only to advance himself at the expense of others. The whole system was Calvinism with God left out.

Sam was so impressed with this reasoning, which he heard all through that winter, that during his next fifty years he built his own philosophy upon it.

By April he had had enough of Cincinnati. He resolved to be off on his pilgrimage. He boarded the *Paul Jones*, bound for New Orleans. The pilot was Mr. Horace Bixby.

4

KING OF THE RIVER

Sam came up to Mr. Bixby and stood a little behind him as he guided the enormous wheel of the *Paul Jones*. Beyond the windows of the pilothouse stretched the shining Ohio, its banks tinted with the green of early spring.

"How would you like a young man to learn the river?" Sam said.

Horace Bixby, a short, hot-tempered, "gunpowdery" man of thirty-two, was one of the best-known pilots of the river—a "lightning" pilot. That April morning he had a sore foot. He did not enjoy having passengers intrude into his pilothouse anyway.

"I wouldn't like it," Mr. Bixby said.

Sam persisted. By way of references he mentioned the Bowen boys, his schoolmates who had become pilots. Mr. Bixby knew and approved of them. He seemed to soften. After a few moments, during which they merely looked at the river, he asked Sam's name.

"What makes you drawl your words so?" Mr. Bixby said.

"You'll have to ask my mother. She drawls hers."

Horace Bixby laughed. "Did you ever do any steering?"

Sam said he had steered everything on the river but a steamboat.

"Take the wheel," Bixby said, "and keep her as she is."

He sat down to rest his foot, never taking his eyes off Sam. In a while he said: "The only way I would take a young man to learn the river is for money. Five hundred dollars."

Sam had fourteen dollars to his name. He offered Bixby some of the Tennessee land, but the pilot was not interested. Sam figured how much he might borrow from his brother-in-law. He made a counteroffer.

"I'll give you one hundred dollars cash, and the rest when I earn it."

Bixby had come to like the young man. He pondered the terms.

When Sam reached New Orleans, he learned that no boat had sailed for the Amazon for a long time and that none was scheduled to go for the next ten or twelve years.

He was not disappointed. From the moment he stepped into the pilothouse of the *Paul Jones,* his proposed trip to Brazil had retreated from the head of his parade of thoughts. Its place was usurped by his old boyhood dream of becoming a river pilot.

The Amazon, he reasoned, was chancy, dangerous, and far away from home and family and friends. He might never find what he was seeking and might never be able to return. What he really wanted was supremacy, authority, mastery of his own fate.

"A pilot in those days," Mark Twain wrote, "was the only unfettered and entirely independent human being that lived in the earth. . . . In truth, every man and woman and child has a master, and worries and frets in servitude; but in the day I write of, the Mississippi pilot had *none*." Even the captain of a steamboat took instructions from his pilot.

Sam returned to Bixby and repeated his plea to be his apprentice. After three days of Sam's pleading, Bixby surrendered and took him along for free on the *Paul Jones*'s upriver trip to St. Louis. There Sam borrowed the money he needed from William Moffett, and signed a contract with Horace Bixby. He was now a cub pilot on the Mississippi River.

Apprenticeship was the only way by which the ranks of the pilots could be kept full. It meant learning to know the river not as a geographical phenomenon but as a capricious deity subject to every conceivable change of temperament. No textbook, no chart, no map would be of any value a month after it had been made. Consequently there were none. Pilots learned by experience and by constant interchanges of information as their boats passed or as they met at landings or in the principal terminals of the steamboat route: New Orleans and St. Louis. A pilot's training was a matter of memory; the river had to become as familiar to him as the hall of his own house, and he had to find his way along it as confidently as he would along that hall in the dark. Not only human lives but hundreds of thousands of dollars' worth of cargo, not to mention the boat itself, depended on the pilot's confidence in his complete knowledge of the river. A pilot never said, "I think"; only, "I know."

Mark Twain compared the task to memorizing every house and window and door and lamppost and sign along both sides of the longest street in New York, and knowing them so well that they could be identified on an inky-black night. Then to relearn them once a month after every one had been changed in position and appearance. Or to knowing the Bible so thoroughly that he could open it at random, and without a mistake recite passages before and after the verse his finger rested on. Such feats, he wrote, were "no marvelous facility compared to a pilot's massed knowledge of the Mississippi and his marvelous facility in the handling of it."

For the twelve-hundred-mile-long, fickle, villainous Mississippi between New Orleans and St. Louis was forever changing her course, and as the water level rose and fell, landmarks disappeared and outlines altered. A shoal might be well covered with water one trip; the next, the channel would have swerved. A promontory or an island would vary its shape; sunken trees would suddenly thrust their dead branches up to clutch at hulls; between trips just enough more silt would be piled up by the current to make a treacherous sandbar; snags were always hunting up new quarters; banks caved in or rose to new heights.

In stretches of the river where the banks were not rocky, the water would cut deep, horseshoe-shaped curves with a perimeter sometimes as long as thirty-five miles. Rascally plantation owners whose land was back from the river would dig ditches through the arms of these horseshoes, thus bringing the river to their property and doubling its value. Then with amazing speed the cutoff would fill up. One of the river legends was of a steamboat trapped on a dark night in such a predicament, and still trying to find its way out. The river had a lore of its own.

For eighteen months Sam Clemens studied the science of the river under Horace Bixby's instruction. Bixby was a hard master, but not an unkind one. He made Sam get a notebook in which to write down every bit of information he gave him orally, and then made him memorize it. The training seemed endless to Sam, because he would be on watch with Bixby only four hours at a stretch.

In time, Sam thought he had learned the river well enough to stand his watch alone. Then one summer day, when he relieved Bixby, the pilot announced that he was going below.

"I suppose you know the next crossing?" Bixby said.

Sam insisted that he could run it with his eyes shut.

"You think so, do you?" Bixby said.

Sam thought it a strange question. He began to wonder whether he did indeed know the depth of the water. Perhaps the river had changed since he last reached the spot. Perhaps Bixby knew this and had counted on Sam's finding it out for himself. The cub began to imagine all sorts of hazards.

He saw the captain come on deck, then the chief mate, then, one by one, the rest of the crew. Bixby was nowhere visible. Sam was alone in the pilothouse, the safety of the boat wholly in his hands.

The captain looked up at him. "Where is Mr. Bixby?" he asked in a worried tone.

Sam's imaginings immediately multiplied. He was sure he saw a shoal ahead. He grew so frightened that he could hardly pull the bell rope, the signal for soundings.

Together the captain and the mate yelled at the leadsman for a quick report on the depth of the water. In a gloomy voice the man answered that the boat was drawing less and less.

Frantically Sam shouted through the speaking tube to the engineer: "Ben, if you love me, *back* her! Quick, Ben! Oh, back the immortal *soul* out of her!"

Then he heard the pilothouse door open and softly close. Bixby stood behind him, a patronizing smile on his face. The crew on the deck were shrieking with laughter.

"Didn't you know there was no bottom in that crossing?" Bixby said.

"Yes, sir, I did."

"Then you shouldn't have allowed me or anybody else to shake your confidence in that knowledge. Try to remember that. And another thing: when you get into a dangerous place, don't turn coward. That isn't going to help matters any."

Sam took the lesson to heart, but he resented the trick that had been pulled on him. Fond of playing practical jokes himself, he was too sensitive to take a teasing. For a long time he had to live with his shipmates' taunting repetition of "Oh, Ben, if you love me, back her!"

At times he got discouraged. Once Bixby deliberately tried to confuse him by predicting how the river would have changed before their next trip. Sam answered his questions correctly, then burst out: "Have I got to keep up an everlasting measuring of the banks of the river, twelve hundred miles, month in and month out?"

"Of course!"

"Then I've got to go to work and learn just as much more river as I already know?"

"Just about twice as much more."

"I think I was a fool when I went into this business," Sam moaned.

"Yes, that is true. You are yet," Bixby said. "But you'll not be when you've learned it."

"I never can learn it."

"I will see that you *do,*" Bixby said.

Eventually he did. At last, on September 9, 1858, Sam was granted a pilot's license. Bixby took him on as a partner. Sam could now advise the captain of one of those splendid boats, so important then to the life of the vast midsection of America.

Steamboating on the Mississippi had begun to flourish after Andrew Jackson's 1815 victory at New Orleans had freed the river from British domination during the War of 1812. Previously, transportation of goods had been on hand-poled flatboats which took nine months to cover the course. In 1816, Henry Miller Shreve's development of an efficient river steamboat, the *Washington*, transformed the commerce of the nation. Now the distance could be covered in less than one-half the time.

Steamboat building became a major industry in the West. The great navigable rivers of the Mississippi Basin joined into one mighty stream connecting the Atlantic Ocean with the Rocky Mountains. By the time Sam Clemens became a pilot, New Orleans was the first port of the country in the value of its exports. The Mississippi steamboats were carrying ten million tons of freight up and down the river—almost twice as much as the foreign trade of the United States.

They also carried hordes of immigrants into the western wilderness to turn it into the food basket of America. And back to the East they carried the reports of the new settlers—reports that became the "tall tales" which were the basis of the lively humor of the young country and which Mark Twain was to exploit. Like the yarns of the mariners of the sixteenth-century era of discovery, who reported that they had heard mermaids singing and seen men whose heads "do grow beneath their shoulders," now tales drifted back of squash vines that grew so fast they chased the hogs squealing from the fields, making the ground shake; and of steamboats that moved so fast the pilots had to swerve from their course to let the lightning go by.

When Sam was a pilot, Mississippi River packets could run the twelve hundred miles between New Orleans and St. Louis in about four days. Being of shallow draft, they could pull up to the landings along the banks to unload goods and load new shipments and to take on wood, their principal fuel. Woodcutting to supply this need became a thriving business in the Mississippi Basin.

The wood was stacked on the bottom deck, where it could be quickly fed into the furnaces that turned the paddle wheels on each side of the boat. These were cased in brightly decorated housings that bore the name of the vessel. Its hull and superstructure were painted white and ornamented with scrollwork.

Two tall smokestacks were the distinctive feature of the packets. Their tops were shaped to resemble a spraying crown of plumes. Between them stretched a pair of lacy, gilded metal strips to brace them. At night the smoke from the chimneys, speckled with sparks, made the boats seem like roving volcanoes.

The pilothouse behind them, "all glass and 'gingerbread,'" was perched on the "texas," or top, deck. Comfortably furnished, it was a clubhouse for officers and visiting pilots. On the next lower deck were staterooms and a long, gilded, glittering salon (or "saloon," at it was then called) for the use of "cabin," or first class, passengers. The lowest deck was for cargo and steerage, or "deck," passengers, whose only shelter was the floor of the deck above. The boats were staffed with a battalion of deckhands, firemen, and roustabouts; and a regiment of stewards and chambermaids. The food was rich and plentiful. An orchestra and sometimes a troupe of actors or minstrels amused the passengers.

Every boat carried a great variety of people. Associating with them and with the other pilots was no small part of Sam's education. Mark Twain would say of this aspect of the river: "I got personally and familiarly acquainted with about all the different types of human nature that are to be found in fiction, biography, or history. . . . When I find a well-drawn character in fiction or biography I generally take a warm personal interest in him, for the reason that I have known him before—met him on the river."

He took part in the moonlight dances on the steamboat decks, and the other parties. He would play the piano at them, and sing his favorite song:

I had an old horse whose name was Methusalem;
Took him down and sold him in Jerusalem.

In the gatherings of pilots he acquired a reputation as a spinner of tall tales. His quaint way of speech amused his audiences as much as the stories themselves did. One of his stories dealt with his presence of mind in saving an old man from the fourth floor of a blazing hotel.

"I yelled for a rope," Sam would drawl. "When it came, I threw the old man the end of it. He caught it, and I told him to tie it around his waist. He did so, and I pulled him down."

The story illustrates not only the nature of the tall tale, but the manner in which one should be told to be successful. The narrator begins with a plausible premise, snares the listener's confidence with even more believable details as he builds up the middle section, then lets him down with an absurd conclusion.

There were also many times when Sam was alone. He was regarded as a great reader, so well informed that his conversation could be as instructive as it was amusing. He began to learn French, writing neat exercises in his pilot's notebook. Perhaps this is what Horace Bixby had in mind when he said that Sam was always scribbling.

Then there were the nights in New Orleans when, from seven to seven, he would guard freight on the wharves to earn three dollars. He would watch the stars and the planets and, awed by the immensity of space and what might lie beyond his eye, would ponder the questions the heavens pose—life, death, eternity, causality, the mysteries of God and fate. Into his pilot's notebook he pasted a newspaper clipping on "How to Take Life." Its sentiments corresponded to his own: "Take it as though you were born to the task of performing a merry part in it—as though the world had awaited for your coming." Its closing sentence he adopted as part of his creed: "The miracle, or the power that elevates the few, is to be found in industry, application, and perseverance under the promptings of a brave, determined spirit."

During most of his life he liked such generalizations. So long as they could be supported with "perpendicular fact," he followed their principles and believed in their optimism. Only much later did he come to see with an embittered eye the ironies they left unsaid.

His own industry, application, and perseverance at the time turned him out a better-than-average river pilot. Many years later, Horace Bixby remembered that Sam lacked confidence. If the recollections of the then old man are correct, the lack can be excused by the fact that Sam was not quite twenty-three when he got his license, and only twenty-five when he quit the river.

The river no longer had a purely romantic appeal for him. "I had lost something which could never be restored to me while I lived," Mark Twain wrote. "All the grace, the beauty, the poetry had gone out of the majestic river." A glorious sunset, something that always thrilled him, came to mean merely a prophecy of what the next day's weather would be. But he had come to love the river by understanding the science of it and mastering the language of the water. Now, for example, he knew whether a distant agitation on its surface meant a shoal or was just a wind ruffle. He thought only of what the features of the river "could furnish toward compassing the safe piloting of a steamboat." Only this love could have turned the impractical, romantic, dreamy Sam Clemens, who hated details, into a pilot who never had an accident.

Plenty of accidents did occur on the river, usually at night; there was no illumination whatever on the river then. A boat could run aground on a shoal or strike a snag. It could hit a flatboat or a raft and sink it with loss of life. For the river, as Mark Twain wrote, "from end to end was flaked with coal fleets and timber rafts, all managed by hand." These carried a crew of two dozen men or more, were topped with wigwams for storm quarters, and were laden with "an acre or so of white, sweet-smelling boards." A fragment of one of these rafts provided Huck Finn and Jim with the transportation for their deathless voyage down the Mississippi. But the worst of the accidents were the fires that could consume the wooden steamboats to the waterline, and the boiler explosions that could shatter them to atoms. Loss of life in the river steamboat trade rose to such proportions that the United States government had to take action to enforce safety measures.

Before Sam Clemens had got his pilot's license he had enticed his brother Henry, who was idling in St. Louis, to follow in his footsteps. He got Henry a job as clerk on the *Pennsylvania.*

As the steamboat schedules changed, Sam shifted from boat to boat. At this time he was the cub for a Mr. Brown, pilot of the *Pennsylvania,* who was famous along the river for his memory, his long-windedness, his tyranny, and his bad temper. Sam and he did not get on well, and Brown played more cruel tricks to test him than Horace Bixby had.

The captain of the *Pennsylvania* sent Henry to Brown with an order to stop at a particular plantation. Brown, who tried to hide his deafness, either did not hear or did not choose to obey the order; at any rate, he passed the landing by. The captain was furious with Brown, who took out his own rage on Henry. He was about to hit the boy with a ten-pound lump of coal when Sam intervened and knocked Brown out cold.

He was haled before the captain for this serious breach of discipline. After hearing Sam's story, the captain reminded Sam that he had been guilty of a great crime, and added: "I'm damn glad of it!" After Sam left the captain's cabin he could hear the man laughing and slapping his thigh.

When the boat reached New Orleans, Sam transferred to the *A. T. Lacey* because of his feud with Brown. Henry remained on the *Pennsylvania.* The night before it left, the brothers sat till midnight on the levee, talking of steamboat disasters. They decided that if one befell them. they should stick to the boat and help as best they might.

Possibly, as they parted, Sam thought of a dream he had had shortly before at Pamela's house in St. Louis. In it he saw Henry lying in a metal coffin that rested on two chairs. A bunch of white flowers with a red one in its center lay on his breast. He told Pamela of the dream, but undoubtedly he did not mention it to his younger brother. He had grown fond and proud of the handsome, attractive twenty-year-old.

When Sam was at Greenville, Mississippi, two days out from New Orleans, he got word that the *Pennsylvania,* which had left New Orleans before the *A. T. Lacey,* had blown up with the loss of one hundred and fifty of the five-hundred-odd lives it carried.

At first Sam thought Henry was safe, but a later bulletin reported the boy hurt beyond help. Sam rushed to Memphis, Tennessee, where the injured had been carried. Henry lay among them in a public hall that had been converted into an emergency hospital staffed with volunteer nurses from among the young ladies of Memphis.

The doctor told Sam that Henry's chances of recovery were good, even though he had inhaled steam and was badly scalded. For two days and nights Sam watched by his brother's bedside. On the sixth day after the explosion Henry began to suffer again.

Sam asked a student doctor to give Henry some morphine, which had just come into use, in order to allay the boy's excruciating pain. The medical student said he had but little experience with that new drug, and refused. Sam overruled him. As Mark Twain wrote: "Pilots came to put all their wishes in the form of commands. It 'gravels' me, to this day, to put my will in the weak shape of a request, instead of launching it in the crisp language of an order."

Henry sank into a deep sleep from which he never awakened.

The ladies of Memphis had raised a fund to provide metal coffins for the victims of the disaster. When Sam went to see Henry's body, it lay in one of these, resting on two chairs. An old woman came in and decorated it with a bouquet of white flowers, in the center of which was a red rose.

Sam was inconsolable. He blamed himself for everything connected with Henry's death: his luring the boy to the riverboat life, his letting him remain alone on the *Pennsylvania*, his overriding the doctor about the morphine. In his agony, Sam confessed all this to Orion after they had buried Henry in Hannibal. He never got over his sense of responsibility for the tragedy. Soon after it he began to look old.

Sam and his contemporaries regarded his dream as prophetic, another manifestation of his gift for clairvoyance that his mother had observed long before. Clearer understanding of human psychology since then has robbed dreams of such superstitious explanations. Sam's dream reveals his unconscious wish that Henry would die. His old feelings of envy of Henry's good behavior and exemplary character, and his jealousy of the outward affection Jane Clemens showed her youngest, survived under Sam's conscious change of attitude toward Henry as both of them matured. It was this guilt that tortured Samuel Clemens then. It would continue to plague him for years to come, until in his old age he could exorcise it and similar feelings about other sad events for which he felt to blame.

The incident of the bouquet is an example of a mental phenomenon called temporary amnesia. In moments of emotional excitement a person can "go blank" for a split second. When that experience is over, what happens immediately after the person is again fully conscious seems to him to have occurred long ago. The bouquet was not part of the original, "prophetic" dream; that merely seemed a good place to put it as Sam in distress recalled the whole episode.

Sam served on many boats in the Mississippi River commerce, including the *City of Memphis,* the largest and most splendid of all. He generally earned two hundred and fifty dollars a month, but toward the end of his river career he was making five hundred as the result of the pilots' having unionized their trade. He had no expenses except when on shore. In St. Louis he stayed with the Moffetts, but in livelier New Orleans he sometimes splurged. At least he recorded one magnificent and expensive dinner there. He had become exuberantly prosperous.

All he wrote during his years on the river was a series of letters published in the New Orleans *Crescent* in January, 1861. These are signed Quintus Curtius Snodgrass. The change in his Cincinnati *nom de plume* indicates the more sophisticated tone of these communications about riverboat life and the tense atmosphere that immediately preceded the outbreak of the Civil War. Quintus Curtius Rufus was a Roman author of a life of Alexander the Great; Rufus, which means "red-haired," may have suggested the name to the auburn-locked Samuel Clemens. The letters, in which there is a good deal of satire of army life, show that Sam had still a long way to go toward literary renown.

More important is a parody he wrote of the pompous,

opinionated paragraphs on river lore and predictions that an old pilot named Isaiah Sellers kept publishing in the New Orleans *Picayune*. Sam's burlesque, signed "Sergeant Fathom," appeared in the New Orleans *True Delta* for May 8–9, 1859. It records an absurd trip down the river in 1763 by a "steamer" with a "Chinese captain and a Choctaw crew," and steered with a window shutter. Sergeant Fathom, "one of the oldest cub pilots on the river," claimed to have helped de Soto discover the Mississippi in 1542. The travesty put an end to Captain Sellers' contributions.

Just after the first Quintus Curtius Snodgrass letter appeared, Louisiana seceded from the Union. On April 12, 1861, the guns of Fort Sumter proclaimed the start of the Civil War. In New Orleans the pilots discussed which side of the conflict they would support. Sam had no strong feelings either way. He hated the idea of war.

He went to St. Louis as a passenger on the *Uncle Sam*. Along the river he could see soldiers drilling. The *Uncle Sam* was one of the last steamboats to make the trip before war closed the river to commercial traffic.

Sam's days as a pilot in the profession he said he loved "far better than any I have followed since" had come to an end. Shortly after the war ended, railroads stole most of the river transportation and trade. By that time Sam Clemens was deeply involved in other matters.

5

A YOUNG MAN GOES WEST

In St. Louis, Sam found that he was much in demand as a war pilot, but he refused to serve.

"I'm not very anxious," he said, "to get up into a glass perch [the pilothouse] and be shot at by either side. I'll go home and reflect on the matter."

He went to Hannibal, which he found was pro-Confederacy and already in the hands of Union Home Guards. Missouri's Governor Claiborne Jackson had called out the state militia to resist them.

More to stick with his former playmates than because of convictions, Sam joined a "battalion" of these old companions. They met in secret to organize, behaving like Tom Sawyer's band of boy brigands. In the whole group of fifteen, thirteen were self-commissioned officers. The other two were privates. Sam was a second lieutenant; there was no first lieutenant. They overlooked no opportunity for playacting that they were marching off to die for states' rights, the noble institution of slavery, and their sweethearts.

The account Mark Twain gave of this Keystone Comedy

Corps, in "The Private History of a Campaign that Failed," is only slightly more farcical than its actual experiences. (He invented the shooting of a soldier to show the horror of war and his distaste for it.) After Sam had been thoroughly drenched by the incessant rain on this camp-out, had developed a boil, had almost been burned to death when the heroes accidentally set fire to a hayloft they were sleeping in, and had sprained his ankle, he quit. But not before he had lost his sense of humor over the joke which had turned against him, and had denounced the whole silly business of this campaign and of war in general.

While Sam waited in hiding for his ankle to mend, Governor Jackson's militia was defeated at Boonville. Sam was in danger of being captured by Union troops. As soon as he could walk, he set off for Keokuk to visit Orion, a staunch Union supporter in a Union state.

For the first and only time in his life, Orion was about to hold a position of some importance and responsibility. Edward C. Bates, with whom he had studied law in St. Louis some twelve years earlier, was now in President Abraham Lincoln's cabinet as Attorney General. Orion applied to him for a job. Bates got him one, at $1,800 a year, as secretary to James W. Nye, whom Secretary of State William H. Seward had just appointed Governor of the newly created Nevada Territory.

Nye had been Police Commissioner in New York, Seward's home state, and manager of Seward's unsuccessful campaign for the Republican Presidential nomination. He now proceeded to pay off political debts with jobs in his new jurisdiction. The staff he sent westward Mark Twain was to christen the "Irish Brigade." Its members copied their leader in the matter of patronage. Orion seems to have been sneaked in under the tent to become, in fact, Secretary of State for Nevada Territory.

Orion was, as usual, out of funds. It was a long trip from Keokuk to Carson City. Sam Clemens, on the other hand, had plenty of money from his piloting. Furthermore, his voluntary retirement from service on either side of the Civil War was not wholly appreciated in the actively partisan Middle West. He was very much at liberty. Possibly Orion himself might need a secretary and could be persuaded to overlook a candidate's previous politics, especially if that candidate would supply the money for the trip to Nevada. Orion was easily convinced.

Orion and Sam sailed down to St. Louis, where they took a boat for the six-day trip up the Missouri River to St. Joseph. There they transferred themselves and their baggage—Orion was lugging along a six-pound dictionary, and they were allowed only twenty-five pounds of baggage each—to the Overland stagecoach. The fare was $150 each. For the next nineteen days, including a two-day stop in Salt Lake City where Sam was not seriously impressed with Mormon ways, they jolted over the plains and mountains, arriving in Carson City on August 14, 1861.

This capital, located in the desert, was a helter-skelter collection of frame houses, stores, offices, and stables, more or less grouped around a central plaza. Its population was around two thousand, mostly prospectors and miners who had heard Nevada was full of riches and had lost no time in getting to them with development capital easily raised in San Francisco.

Carson City was prospering as few other new settlements have thrived before or since. All the talk was about the mines, and the treasure they held. Almost every week a new deposit of gold or silver, antimony, mercury, or cement was discovered where only sand and sagebrush had been before. People went to bed paupers, and awoke nabobs. Shares, or "feet," in the claims "that went begging yesterday were worth a brick house today," So Mark Twain wrote in *Roughing It*, his account of the years he spent in the West. And "cartloads of solid silver bricks, as large as pigs of lead, were arriving from the mills every day."

There was plenty of drinking and gambling and shooting, too, for there was no law in the Territory. When the Clemens brothers arrived in Carson City, one of the welcoming committee excused himself to rebuke a stranger who had accused him of helping rob the California coach. After each had emptied his pistols, the welcomer nodded a polite good-bye to Sam and rode home, blood from his wounds dripping all over his horse. The "favorite place of resort" in Carson City was the Magnolia Saloon, rivaled only by the Golden Age Dance Hall, which featured the spirited Emma Pastor.

Sam thought little of his new environment, where it never rained and the dew never fell and the sand and alkali dust were everywhere. Nor of his new neighbors—"thieves, murderers, desperadoes . . . Indians, Chinamen, Spaniards, gamblers, sharpers, coyotes, poets, preachers and jackass rabbits." It was, he wrote Pamela, a place that "would make the devil homesick for hell." He himself was homesick for the woods and streams of the East.

Organizing the Territory into a semblance of order was no easy task. Governor Nye did not take his duties very seriously. He was not even in Nevada when the Clemens brothers arrived, for he had left his papers of authority behind in New York and had had to go to pick them up in San Francisco, to which port they had been forwarded by boat. Orion had to manage, and he was too honest to please Nye. Nye's idea of justifying the presence of the Irish Brigade was to give them jobs surveying a railroad; they were not to stop until they reached the Atlantic Ocean, then were to bridge it and move on. Nye objected to Orion's criticism of these and other expenditures of United States government money. Sam took Orion's side and rebuked Nye so forcefully that Orion was not troubled again. The governor seems to have respected Sam for this defense of the family integrity.

Thereafter Orion was careful to consult Sam about issues that had to be decided when Orion was Acting Governor during Nye's absences, which were frequent. As a result, Sam had a certain influence on the development of Nevada. He had small interest in affairs of state, however. His duties as Orion's secretary were few, and he got no pay for performing them.

He spent most of his first days in the plaza, lolling against a post of the Ormsby House, scrutinizing the passersby, gathering the news and gossip, vaguely planning to move on beyond the Rockies to see the rest of the country. When the weather grew colder, his office became a gathering place for other exiles like himself, the members of Nye's Irish Brigade who boarded with him at the establishment of a Mrs. Murphy (Mrs. O'Flannigan in *Roughing It*), who had followed Governor Nye from New York. Sam would loll by the stove, drawling tales of the Mississippi River hour after hour, and delighting his audience. In bustling Carson City he got a reputation for indolence, charming though it was. Orion, on the other hand, was busy as a bureaucrat, trying to save the government's money and ending up by having to pay for a lot of things himself.

Sam had landed in Carson City with $800. Out of this he had to keep both himself and Orion, whose paycheck, like most obligations of a bureaucracy, was slow in arriving. In addition, Sam had spent a sizable sum on the "Mexican Plug" he had been duped into buying. This untamed and untamable animal, totally unsuited for anything but horsemeat, quickly consumed hay at a cost of $250 a ton. Sam was not entirely free of the family trait of investing in attractive but impractical projects.

It came time for Sam to "see the elephant"—the local phrase for the get-rich-quick vision which infected almost everyone who had come to that dreary land. He had discarded the finery of a Mississippi pilot's costume, which made him conspicuous in Nevada, for the slouch hat, blue flannel shirt, coarse, baggy pants, and heavy boots of the pioneer. And he had removed his pilot's sideburns and grown a mustache. But he had by no means adjusted himself otherwise to the ways of the frontier. He was pathetically, even ludicrously, unskilled in how to go about making the fortune he now not only needed, but craved. He approached prospecting with the same romanticism with which, as a boy, he had dug for treasure around Hannibal.

Sam had to be in Carson City for the opening on October 1 of the first Territorial Legislature. Consequently, he decided first to exploit the treasures aboveground. With John Kinney, a rich Ohioan's son, he set off for Lake Tahoe to stake out a claim on the timberland around its shores. On the treeless Nevada plain any wood was in great demand; a cord of it brought $40 on the inflated market of the frontier.

The two young men turned the expedition into a glorious camping trip of about three weeks. Sam found the lake even more beautiful than it had been described to him—he made it a criterion for the scenery he was to see in many parts of the world—and he reveled in the bracing air of the high, primeval forest. But he was so green a woodsman that he let his campfire get out of control one evening. It started a forest fire that reduced the timber on their claim to charcoal. For four hours he and John Kinney just watched the blaze and its reflection in the lake. Then a storm blew up and mercifully put an end to the conflagration—and the expedition.

The legislature convened on the outskirts of Carson

City in a house that had been provided at the last moment by one of the richest miners in the region. Since the Nevadans were not too pleased with the outsiders who had been sent to administer their Territory, they had offered no housing for the legislature, which they did not want. Also provided were pine benches for the legislators, and sawdust for the floors "by way of carpet and spittoon combined." Such are the ways of bureaucracy, however, that Orion's salary was docked for the rent he was supposed to pay for what the government was getting free.

Most of the legislators sat with their feet on their desks, munching raw turnips and spitting on the floor—both then common habits which astonished and disgusted European visitors more than any other American custom. It was hard for Sam to take the legislature's rowdy sessions seriously. He saw through the politicians' pretensions to their conceit, their egotism, and their dishonesty. They were poor specimens of what he had imagined legislators to be and of what he thought they should be. The humorous articles he wrote about them brought him to the attention of Joseph T. Goodman, editor of the *Daily Territorial Enterprise*, published in Virginia City. At that time it was the most influential newspaper in the West.

Not until the legislature adjourned in December, 1861, could Sam get away from Carson City to do any real prospecting. By that time new strikes of gold, silver, and mercury in Humboldt County were reported as bringing in ore worth $7,000 a ton. Even in those days of fantastic fortunes made overnight this was electrifying news. Gold Hill, near Carson City, yielded only $20 to $40 a ton, and was the most successful silver region in Nevada. Immediately Sam teamed up with three other inexperienced Easterners and set off one chilly afternoon on the two-hundred-mile trip northward to the new Golconda.

It took them fifteen days to reach Unionville. They had

walked and pushed most of the way because their horses proved unequal to the task of hauling both provisions and equipment, and their owners.

Day after day they went prospecting, until one of them who had some knowledge of geology declared they had "found it!" They staked out claims and went to work with pick and shovel, later with a drill and blasting powder. After a week Sam, who was not physically equipped to be a miner, quit. They tried tunneling, but quit again. Finally they understood that the easy way to wealth was not to do the mining themselves, but to sell their claims at a staggering profit on the strength of ore samples, and let the new owners do the digging.

The party split up, each to go his separate way. After almost losing his life once in a flash flood, again in a tavern full of drunken rowdies, and once more in a snowstorm, Sam reached Carson City. Except by experience, he was no richer than when he had left two months before.

He was not through with prospecting, though, and planned to return to Humboldt. In the meantime he thought it advisable to inspect the claims in Esmeralda County, in which he and Orion had invested. So far, they had got no return on their money—only demands for more to develop the mines. Sam's own funds were almost exhausted. Orion had to stake the expedition.

Sam got to Aurora, about one hundred miles south of Carson City, in mid-February, to find the ground frozen and covered with snow, and the Clemens' claims absolutely worthless.

He resolved to stay, nevertheless, and was presently joined by Calvin Higbie, with whom he shared a little cabin. To beguile the tedium of inactivity caused by the bad weather, Sam began writing letters to the *Enterprise* about life in Aurora.

Until the winter broke up, the only diversion in the camp was the gambling saloon and dance hall. Sam went to the square-dance "balls" and enjoyed himself like a child. If he could not follow the figures, he danced by himself and in his own style, to the vast amusement of the rest of the company. All the ladies were dying to have him as a partner.

In the spring, Sam and Higbie began work on various claims, hoping to sell them, but finding no purchasers. Finally Sam was so broke that he worked as a common laborer in a stamping mill. He gave up the job after a week, having by then found that it cost him more to live than he was being paid. He had caught a terrible cold and was almost salivated by the mercury used in getting gold and silver from the quartz.

At last he and Higbie discovered a blind lead, and claimed it. It began to look as if they would be the millionaires they dreamed of becoming. They made wild plans for the houses they would build, the trips they would take, and the debts they would pay. They refused all offers to buy their claims.

Then Sam was summoned to help nurse Captain Nye, brother of the governor, who was seriously ill at his ranch nine miles away. He left a note for Higbie. Ten days later he returned on foot to find a disconsolate partner. Not knowing of Sam's departure, Higbie had thrown a note through the cabin window, warning Sam to be sure to work the claim within ten days. Then Higbie himself had left on another project. They had lost the claim for failure to work it within the specified time. The hours Sam had spent walking home and stopping to help a woman whose husband had been seized with epilepsy would have saved their fortune.

Much later they learned that the blind lead had proved practically worthless.

Sam made one last effort with Higbie, but his lack of skill in digging a shaft wore out his patience. Like his father, Sam could not "dig in the streets." He returned to the cabin in utter misery, disgusted with what he called his "slothful, valueless, heedless career" for the past twenty-six years. Eventually he recovered himself sufficiently to open the letter he had picked up at the post office on his way home. It was an offer of $25 a week to go to Virginia City and be city editor of the *Enterprise*.

A week before, Sam would have laughed at the offer. Now it seemed a gift from heaven, though, in his less hopeful days, he had made some effort to solicit it. Accepting it, however, meant that he would have to leave off prospecting and abandon his dreams of sudden wealth. On the other hand, if he did not take it up, he would have to be dependent on others. The very thought of that shamed him. For several days he debated the issue, then squared his shoulders and set out on foot to cover the one hundred and thirty miles from Aurora to Virginia City.

It was a hot August afternoon when, looking rather rusty, he walked into the office of the *Daily Territorial Enterprise*.

"My name is Clemens," he said, "and I've come to write for the paper."

Editor-in-chief Joseph Goodman was away at the time. It was William Wright, known throughout the West by his pen name "Dan De Quille," who took Sam in hand. Dan was an Ohioan, six years Sam's senior, and the *Enterprise*'s star mining reporter until the paper folded in 1890. He had liked Sam's letters to the *Enterprise* about the ludicrous legislators in Carson City, and gave him a warm welcome.

When Goodman returned, he gave Sam instructions. "Go all over town and ask all sorts of people all sorts of questions. Make notes of the information gained, and write them out for publication." Then he added: "Never say 'We learn' so-and-so, or 'It is reported,' or 'It is rumored,' or 'We understand' so-and-so, but go to headquarters and get the absolute facts, and then speak out and say 'It *is*' so-and-so. Otherwise, people will not put confidence in your news. Unassailable certainty is the thing that gives a newspaper the firmest and most valuable reputation."

Sam was starting his first job as a real reporter on a real newspaper. No reporter before or since could have got better advice.

On the day of his debut, Sam was uncovering little he thought newsworthy. Then a desperado killed a man in a saloon, and was promptly hanged. Sam was unspeakably grateful to the villain. Now, what with a few less dramatic items, he soon had filled the two columns assigned to him.

If he had thought Carson City lawless, Sam found Virginia City wide open and never closed. It was situated at the foot of Mount Davidson, which contained the Comstock Lode, an extraordinarily rich deposit of gold and silver. Sam had hit Virginia City when the Lode was at its height of wealth-producing ore.

As elsewhere in Nevada, men were becoming millionaires overnight. Business was booming, and prices soared. All supplies had to be imported in wagons invented by the Studebaker who later would extend his name and fortune by inventing a make of automobile. Houses of from one to three stories clustered on the hill slopes, sheltering many strata of society, the lowest of which was the Chinese. The society was almost wholly masculine. The few wives and daughters were honored; the many "fallen women" were ignored publicly. Through the streets occasionally stalked a troupe of camels, pathetic remnants of a herd imported as potential beasts of burden; they could not adapt to the stones and harsh alkalies of the American desert, and died out in misery.

The city was a veritable metropolis. It boasted three stock exchanges, where claims were bought and sold. It supported four churches, four newspapers, public and private schools, three theaters, and forty-two saloons.

C Street was the most famous of Virginia City's thoroughfares. Here were the International Hotel, opposite which was the *Enterprise* office, the Wells Fargo depot, the Assay and Recorder offices. Here, too, were the most popular saloons: the Sazerac, the Sawdust Corner, and the Bucket of Blood. A saloonkeeper ranked with a lawyer or a banker in the social scale, providing he had gained the prestige of having "killed his man."

Life was cheap in Virginia City. The story was that the first twenty-six graves in its cemetery were occupied by murdered men. Many more were to be similarly filled. Little provocation was needed for a pistol to bark. If there was any investigation of the legality of the action, it was a farce; juries made up of illiterates and desperadoes always brought in a verdict of Not Guilty. Usually the farce was dispensed with; if the citizens were sufficiently outraged by a shooting, or considered it palpably unjustified, they quickly applied the hemp treatment to its perpetrator.

Mark Twain's *Roughing It* vividly and artistically depicts this climate, which was so far from the normal conduct of society elsewhere as to appear humorous beyond belief. One had either to laugh at it or die of despair over it. His reporting is not complete simply because there were too many shootings to be covered at once. It is all too accurate so far as it goes, however, as research has proved.

The funeral of Buck Fanshaw, for example, so brilliantly animated in Chapter 47 of *Roughing It*, was an actual occurrence. The real Buck Fanshaw was Tom Peaseley, proprietor of the Sazerac Saloon. He was a giant of a man from New York City who preferred to make a fortune by keeping the secrets that passed over his bar rather than by mining. The minister in the story was the Reverend Franklin S. Rising, a young, saintly, and courageous preacher from Philadelphia. He was a good friend of Sam Clemens. After a short stay, Mr. Rising had to retire from Nevada because of overwork and strain. Sam met him again a few years later in Hawaii.

One of the biggest bonanzas in these flush times in Virginia City was the *Enterprise* itself. It charged two dollars for a subscription, and whatever it wished for advertisements; and its profits were carried home in buckets. It initiated the literary movement of the West, which was to flourish in the next forty years, producing Bret Harte, Joaquin Miller, Jack London, and Mark Twain.

Sam had rapidly progressed on the *Enterprise* from mere reporting to writing feature material, such as letters from Carson City on the deliberations of the legislature. One of these, dated February 2, 1863, was the first piece ever to bear the famous signature "Mark Twain."

His previous communications, which had been widely reprinted in the West, were signed "Josh," but he disliked that pseudonym. In justifying the change, he said to Goodman: "It is an old river term, a leadsman's call, signifying two fathoms—twelve feet. It was always a pleasant sound for a pilot to hear on a dark night. It meant safe water."

Later he was to say that he adopted it out of respect to old Captain Isaiah Sellers, who had thus signed his fatuous opinions about the Mississippi, and whose literary career Sam Clemens had blasted with his "Sergeant Fathom" parody. But Isaiah Sellers never used any *nom de plume*. Either Sam in his old age forgot the origin of the name or he wished to conceal his true reasons for taking it.

One reason is that he had not lost his love for the river, and hankered to return to it. Many years later, when he was a rich and famous author, he told his close friend William Dean Howells that he "would drop everything for a chance to go piloting again." The new pen name would always remind him of the profession he had loved and lost.

Another reason lies in the words of his explanation to Goodman. Sam had been through a "dark night" of homesickness, self-doubt, disgust at his wasted years, financial ruin, loss of his hopes, Now, on the *Enterprise*, he was finding himself as a journalist admired and befriended by his colleagues and chief, whom he in turn respected. Furthermore, his family and social ties were strengthened by the arrival in Nevada of Orion's wife Mollie, who soon afterward became the leader of Carson City society. Here was a new life that had a "safe sound." It required a new identity to go with it.

The causes for this need go deep. Now that the world was beginning to accept Sam Clemens for what he himself was, his own love of life and the world responded. A human being learns to love only by being loved. Up to this time, Sam had experienced rejection and disappointment. Now recognition of himself as a person was stimulating the flow of love his past experiences had held in check. He was becoming pleased with himself and with what he saw around him. His own personality was growing important to him. He could see that it had to be served.

"Mark Twain" represents the new and positive personality which had been struggling in Samuel Clemens to be born. But the personality of the outcast Samuel Clemens still existed with all its guilt-ridden fears and negative attitudes. It always would exist. The combination of the two personalities made the man dynamic in the same way that a positive and a negative pole exist apart in the same dry cell to produce a vital spark when brought into contact with each other.

After Mark Twain put his entire being into what he was doing, the effect was electric. The charge could not be wasted; it had to be connected. He had to have an audience whose response to the current would in turn enliven him. In those Comstock days he was discovering this power within himself and learning to use it.

Years later, when he had begun to understand this division of personality, he searched for means of expressing it. His gropings tend to clarify the problem. For example, he tried a freak for a symbol—a human creature of one trunk and one pair of legs, but with two heads and two pairs of arms. Each of the heads took control of the body and the legs for a week at a time, and each was quite different from the other. The attempt, *Those Extraordinary Twins,* is a failure. It took Mark Twain a long time to find a satisfactory symbol.

The change did not happen all at once. It would be years before it became clearly noticeable. For the time being, he devoted his efforts to inventing the kind of rough humor then popular in the West.

It was popular because it covered up the deep loneliness of the exiles. Their personal ties to home and family were severed; their hopes were as likely dashed as realized; their old standards were meaningless. It was not deep humor, or penetrating, or loving; such exists only when people are in tune with their environment. Instead it was —when not actually cruel—sentimental, in a way which is a disguise for cruelty. The miners were a sentimental lot. One offered a hundred dollars in gold dust for permission to kiss a baby. *East Lynne,* possibly the most sentimental play of all time, was a favorite in Virginia City. But, best of all, these outcasts loved the story that tested their own experience and quickness of intelligence—the hoax.

Mark Twain invented two splendid examples of this

kind of humor. One reported the discovery of a petrified man. It was a burlesque on the mania for finding relics of a past civilization in an area where everything was painfully new, but it was executed so skillfully that it was fully believed and copied in hundreds of papers, even in London. Lost to most readers in the mass of plausible details was the item that the stone man was double-thumbing his nose.

The other, the "Empire City Massacre," was written to expose and condemn the mine owners' vicious system of "cooking" dividends to increase the value of their stock, then selling out and leaving the gullible purchasers ruined. The story, which for credibility centers around the Magnolia Saloon, tells of a man who had murdered his wife and nine children and then committed suicide, as a result of insanity brought on by his having been swindled by cooked dividends. There were plenty of clues to the hoax in the story, but it was so close to what might have happened in that wild country that it was widely believed and became the talk of the territory.

"Most of the citizens," Mark Twain wrote, "dropped gently into it [the hoax] at breakfast, and they never finished the meal." The details are indeed enough to banish a sensitive appetite.

As Mark's reputation increased on the strength of his writing, he became one of the most prominent features of Virginia City, one of the sights of the town. At first, he lived with everyone else connected with the *Enterprise*, in a shanty on A Street. This was a combination dining hall and bunkhouse, with the bunks hanging in tiers around the walls as on a ship. In an attached shed, "Old Joe," supposedly the best Chinese cook on the Lode, prepared tasty but quite unsanitary meals. Visitors' guts were tested with stomach-turning tales of Old Joe's recipes and ingredients. Here Mark Twain, in self-protection, learned to interpret such subjects as vomit and the stench of decomposing bodies as intrinsically funny.

When mice were found in Old Joe's lard barrels, Mark and Dan De Quille moved out of the bunkhouse and took quarters on North C Street, which they equipped with fancy furniture imported from San Francisco. Mark's salary had been raised to $40 a week. Their place became a rendezvous for their friends. They were all very merry, and elaborate practical jokes were the order of those gay days.

Mark had not yet learned to take a joke on himself, and would fly into a rage at so harmless a one as having the candles hidden from him. When he discovered that the ceremony his friends arranged for the public presentation to him of a "valuable" meerschaum pipe in honor of his literary achievements was a fraud, and the pipe a fake, his feelings were sorely hurt. This joke had been concocted by Steve Gillis, the diminutive young typesetter on the *Enterprise*. Mark was fond of the boy, who in some ways took the place of Henry in his affections.

Virginia City's theaters attracted many well-known performers. Among them was thin, tubercular Artemus Ward (Charles Farrar Browne), the most famous humorous lecturer of his day. Ward visited Virginia City in December, 1863, and liked it so much that he stretched his intended stay of a few days to three weeks. He saw that he and Mark were two of a kind, and they became inseparable companions. The first two weeks were riotous ones. They reached a climax after a magnificent Christmas Eve dinner at the city's elegant French restaurant, Chaumond's, with Mark and Artemus walking on the roofs of the houses. Then the party went on for another week.

Ward encouraged Mark in his writing, saying that he expected great things of his new friend. He recommended

Mark to the editor of the New York *Sunday Mercury*, which accepted a few of his submissions.

This encouragement started Mark's feet to itching again. A pleasure trip to San Francisco had introduced him to some of its literary people. Several of his letters were published in the San Francisco *Morning Call.* He was beginning to think Virginia City offered him no more worlds to conquer. Then the death from spotted fever of Orion's little daughter Jennie, on February 1, 1864, saddened him. She was a sweet child whom Mark loved. She had been saving pennies from her pocket money toward a Bible for the Carson City church.

Nevertheless, Mark's services as correspondent for the legislature were much in demand. The Nevadans wanted statehood under a constitution, so that they could get rid of Nye and his corrupt politicians. When this constitution was finally adopted, the legislators rewarded Mark for his help with a $200 watch weighing one pound.

The constitution established two houses of the legislature. As soon as the session adjourned, the journalists of Nevada, for the benefit of a church, got up a show in which they burlesqued the meetings of the self-satisfied lawmakers. They called it "The Third House." Since Mark Twain had not reported the sessions of the legislature very admiringly, the journalists unanimously elected him to deliver the "Governor's Message" to their mock assembly. They were honoring him for having become the most feared political writer in Nevada. The message was the first of the hundreds of humorous speeches he was to make.

Then the mines started to decline, and Orion, due to his incorrigible vacillation, lost the job he could have had in the new state. Mark's growing dissatisfaction led him into an imprudent feud with a Mr. James Laird, editor of the rival *Union.*

It started when Mark was acting editor of the *Enterprise* during Goodman's absence. In a scathing editorial Mark implied that Laird was misusing the funds raised by the auction of a sack of flour for the benefit of the Sanitary Fund, the Red Cross of the Civil War. It was in incredibly poor taste. Soon personal insults were being exchanged which, by the Virginia City code, had to be wiped out in blood.

Mark was persuaded to challenge Laird to a duel at sunrise. He appointed Steve Gillis his second. Mark had no skill whatever with a pistol; in fact, he was terrified of one. To show Mark how to use the weapon, Steve aimed at a small bird and brought it down at thirty yards.

Just then Laird arrived for the duel, and asked who had killed the bird and at what distance.

"Why, Mark, of course!" Steve Gillis said. "He can do it every time."

Laird's second drew him aside. "You don't want to shoot it out with a man like that. It would be suicide."

Laird offered Mark an apology that was immediately accepted.

But a law had just been passed making a duel a penitentiary offense for both principal and second. It was to be rigidly enforced.

Quickly Mark Twain and Steve Gillis decided on a visit to San Francisco. On May 29, 1864, the California stage carried them away from the place Mark said had given him "the most vigorous enjoyment of life" he had ever experienced.

Mark Twain had found no treasure under the hills and deserts of Nevada; he had found it in himself. A new world was beckoning in which he might spend it.

6

AN INNOCENT GOES ABROAD

Mark Twain was a wanderer again.

The fugitives from justice went straight to the offices of the *Morning Call* in San Francisco. Each was hired: Gillis as a compositor, Mark Twain as a reporter. They lived together, moving their lodgings every month in search of a neighborhood quiet enough for Mark, who was sensitive to noise.

He did not really like San Francisco, and he liked working for the *Call* less. The city was too big for him to get the intimate understanding of it he needed for the kind of sympathetic articles he could write best. The *Call* was too big an organization to let him show individuality. Mere reporting was drudgery to him.

He was not being noticed as he had been in Nevada. The only way he could get attention was to pull a joke like fanning a policeman asleep on his beat with a cabbage leaf until he had attracted a hilarious crowd.

A redeeming feature of the city was a group of budding writers that centered around two literary weeklies, *The Golden Era* and *The Californian*. Their leader was Bret

Harte. Mark Twain had fallen in with him when Harte occupied an office in the same building as the *Call.*

Harte had considerable influence on Mark Twain as a writer. Harte showed him how, out of the bizarre life of the West, a plausible, well-constructed story with genuine humor emerging from the characters themselves could be made. The stories Mark produced during this California period show an advance in maturity and skill over such exaggerated, one-dimensional, unsubtle pieces as the hoaxes he had concocted for the *Enterprise.*

Harte introduced Mark to the group of writers who met in the offices of the *Era.* Besides Mark Twain and Bret Harte, the best known was the poet Joaquin Miller. They were all young; they had aspirations; and they did a good deal to encourage and stimulate one another. Above all, they were free souls and content. The more Mark associated with them and envied the freedom they enjoyed as individuals and as writers, the more discontented he became with the *Call.* The more time he spent with his bohemian new friends, the faster he thought he could grow in the direction he wanted.

He was, in fact, doing very little for the *Call.* He had wangled an assistant with the improbable name of Smiggy McGlural, whom he trained to do most of the reporting while he himself wrote for the *Era* or passed his time in its offices or in Harte's. Soon the paper fired him.

At once he made a deal with Joseph Goodman to write a daily letter about San Francisco for the *Enterprise.* Bret Harte, who had just been made editor of *The Californian,* signed him on to the staff.

In the letters to the *Enterprise,* Mark Twain appears more as a social critic and a reformer than as a literary artist. Except for attacking Nevada judges for "selling" decisions, he had done little before in this field. Now he exposed the corruption in San Francisco's municipal administration—particularly in the police department—and the inhuman way in which the Chinese were treated.

The chief of police let it be known that he had small use for the author of these letters.

Just at this time Steve Gillis who, like many persons of his small stature, was rather aggressive, attacked and somehow managed to beat up a burly barkeeper. He was arrested. Then, after posting bail, he hurried back to Virginia City. When Gillis did not appear for trial, Mark Twain, who had signed the bail bond, was at the mercy of the vindictive police chief.

Almost by divine intervention, Steve's brother Jim arrived in San Francisco and snatched Mark back with him to his log cabin in Jackass Gulch, the pocket-mining region of Tuolumne County. Mark arrived on December 4, 1864, and spent the next three months there with Jim, his "pard" Dick Stoker, and Jim's younger brother Billy. After the bustle of San Francisco, the gulch, "that serene and reposeful and dreamy and delicious sylvan paradise," as Mark Twain recalled it, refreshed his spirit and confirmed him in his new approach to life.

Jim Gillis was an uncultivated genius who could invent marvelous stories that he would tell before the fire as if they were historical fact. Two of these Mark Twain adapted into his own books: the outrageous play the King and the Duke put on in *Huckleberry Finn,* and the attempt of the bluejay to fill up a whole house with acorns in *A Tramp Abroad.*

Jim Gillis had a great influence on Mark Twain. For the recent frantic fortune hunter there was something instructive in the example of Jim and his pard, who had scratched for gold for eighteen years and were just as happy without having found it as they might have been with a bonanza.

As a matter of fact, Mark's feverish thirst for gold had

not entirely left him, and he did some placer mining with his companions in nearby Angel's Camp on the Stanislaus River in Calaveras County. It was the rainy season, and Mark's job of carrying sloshing pails of water added to his continual cold wetness. As in the digging back in Nevada, he concluded that the game was not worth the effort. He preferred to spend his time in the rundown local tavern.

There he met up with an old Illinois river pilot named Ben Coon, who would drone endless stories to whoever would listen. Without once smiling, he launched into one about a miner who had a frog that outjumped all competitors until a rival frog owner filled it so full of shot that it could not budge. The story, and the deadpan way in which it had been told, amused Mark and Jim Gillis, and they adapted the dialogue into their own conversation. Mark jotted the main points of the story into his notebook.

The weather grew worse, and Mark got colder and wetter. He refused to carry another pail of water.

Jim Gillis posted a thirty-day claim, and they trudged back through a snowstorm to Jackass Gulch and the cozy cabin. Before any of them returned to work the claim, it had been seized by some Austrians, who took about twenty thousand dollars' worth of nuggets out of it.

By now, the heat was off Mark in San Francisco, and he returned to its competitive life to resume his muckraking letters to the *Enterprise*. Awaiting his arrival was a letter from Artemus Ward, asking for a contribution to a volume of Western stories Ward was compiling. Mark sent his version of the jumping frog story he had heard in Calaveras County.

Before the manuscript arrived in New York, Ward's book had gone to press. But Ward liked the story so much that he gave it to Henry Clapp, editor of the weekly *Saturday Press*, who was in need of good material to save his sheet from folding. Clapp printed it in the November

18, 1865, issue under the title of "Jim Smiley and His Jumping Frog." It was Mark's first piece of real fiction.

The story was an instantaneous success. Papers everywhere copied it. The name of Mark Twain became famous, and for a long time was always associated with the "Jumping Frog." A professor of Greek even condensed it and used it as a translation exercise in a textbook of that language, pretending it was an ancient Attic fable. For a long time Mark Twain believed that hoax.

The story was later retitled "The Celebrated Jumping Frog of Calaveras County." It was not a new one; long before Mark Twain heard it, it had been circulating around the mining camps. In his hands, however, it became a piece of classic folklore. But Mark was annoyed that what he called "a villainous backwoods sketch" should have brought him his first real fame and made him a national literary figure.

Mark had been invited to go on a tour of the Sandwich Islands, as Hawaii was then called, but the burden of the *Enterprise* assignment kept him from accepting. He was disappointed, and angry at being such a wage slave. Determined to get there somehow, he proposed to the editors of the Sacramento *Union* that their paper send him as a special correspondent to report on Hawaii. They agreed, knowing that Mark Twain material was now an asset to any publication.

Mark thoroughly enjoyed the beautiful islands and the leisurely life of their inhabitants, but his letters for the *Union* are little more than detached, objective reportage. To read these—some of which he included at the end of *Roughing It,* written about himself—is to understand how necessary it was for his best work to develop out of his involvement with the subject. The letters did add to his reputation in California, however.

So did the scoop he filed on the survivors of the shipwrecked *Hornet,* who had spent forty-three days at sea in an open boat. They reached Honolulu while Mark was sick in bed with one of his frequent attacks of boils. He had himself carried on a cot to the hospital where the survivors had been interned, and wrote up the story overnight in order to get it on the ship sailing for the States the next morning. Such an incident was rarer then than now, and the story of the *Hornet* disaster, with Mark Twain's byline, was telegraphed everywhere.

After the enchanted islands of Hawaii, San Francisco seemed drearier than ever to Mark. He grew so depressed that he seriously thought of suicide. He wanted to get away again, to wander purely for the sake of wandering —anything to allay his tortured spirit, still groping for expression.

On his return from his ambassadorship to China, Anson Burlingame had called on Mark while he was still sick in bed. Burlingame praised him, and predicted great things for him if only Mark would refine his style and cultivate people of refinement. His visit flattered Mark, and he took Burlingame's advice very seriously. The visit was a turning point in his literary life and, to a certain extent, in his personal life as well.

The *Union* letters show Mark's first attempts to follow Burlingame's advice, but he believed that to really improve he must polish his provincialism with experiences in older and more civilized regions than the Far West. He wanted to go around the world. But where could he find the money?

It occurred to him that one source of money might be lectures on his Hawaiian expedition. Public lectures then were a popular form of entertainment. In places where there was no theater, opera, or concerts, they were the only proper entertainment. The so-called respectable audiences liked them because they offered instruction as well as pleasure. Lecturers earned fortunes on the various circuits. They ranged from the morally elevating Ralph Waldo Emerson to the merely witty Artemus Ward. Lecturing was a hard field to crack, and all but one of Mark Twain's friends discouraged him.

The one was Colonel John McComb, editor of the *Alta California*, a San Francisco newspaper. "Go ahead," McComb told Mark. "Take the largest house in town, and charge a dollar a ticket."

Mark was almost paralyzed with fright.

Tom Maguire, who owned several theaters in San Francisco, endorsed McComb's enthusiasm, and rented Mark Twain his opera house at half price—fifty dollars, payable in advance. After spending $150 of his own money on publicity, Mark suffered even greater terror.

The posters he ordered advertised that "the absurd customs and characteristics of the natives" of the Sandwich Islands would be "duly discussed and described," thus implying that Mark would dwell on the Hawaiians' nakedness, which he had mentioned rather prudishly in his *Union* letters. Also:

A SPLENDID ORCHESTRA
is in town but has *not* been engaged
ALSO
A DEN OF FEROCIOUS WILD BEASTS
will be on exhibition in the next block
Doors open at 7 o'clock   The Trouble to begin at 8 o'clock

In spite of Mark's fears, the opera house was full. And in spite of his wobbling knees he managed to get the audience with him and never let it go until he had finished, to their hearty applause. He had discovered a medium of expression that was to prove richer than all the veins of gold and silver he had not found. From then on, his career as a speaker always in demand kept pace with, and sometimes outran, his success as an author.

He learned that he could attract as much attention with his personality in a big hall as he could in a barroom, a boarding-house parlor, or a log cabin. On a stage his drawling voice, his slouching posture, and his slovenly gait released an audience's tensions. He was relaxing for them, who could not relax themselves. In the same way, his disrobing of pretentiousness and his outrageous wit did for them what they wanted to, but could not, do for themselves because they had neither the courage nor the intelligence.

Many of Mark Twain's choicest stories had less success in print than on the lecture platform, because there he could verbalize them. In dramatizing himself, he made these tales come alive. For example, the old ghost story of "The Golden Arm," which Mark had heard in his childhood from Uncle Dan'l on the Quarles farm, thrilled his audiences when he told it, but is tame when only read.

All the tricks and devices Mark had acquired by long practice as a raconteur in private, he transferred to his public appearances. He had an instinctive gift for timing, without which any speech or story is ruined, and he learned how to adjust it from a small group to a large one. However spontaneous his lectures seemed, they had been written out in advance. There were a few early mistakes—he once wrecked a lecture by laughing at one of his own jokes he had just invented, and on another occasion spoiled his timing by seeing a new chance for ridicule. After that he planned not only his subject matter but his delivery, calculating a pause for effect down to the last split second, and never introducing anything on the inspiration of the moment. His lectures often showed greater craftsmanship than his writing.

The first San Francisco lecture grossed $1,200, but with

Orion-like mismanagement, Mark Twain had only about $400 to keep for himself. If he was to make the money he wanted, as this initial success indicated he could, he needed a manager. He found one in Denis McCarthy, a former associate on the *Enterprise,* who was in San Francisco at the time. McCarthy arranged for a lecture tour of the West.

When Mark reached Virginia City on this tour, the people welcomed him as one of their own. He was urged to appear again, but he begged off on the excuse that as yet he had prepared only the lecture he had already given.

Steve Gillis, however, was determined that Mark Twain should return. Steve arranged for several of Mark's old friends to disguise themselves, intercept the coach bringing Mark back from a lecture in Carson City, and rob him.

The highwaymen had to wait for hours on a freezing cold night for the coach to appear, but they pulled the robbery off successfully. Mark was calm, even witty, during its progress. He pleaded to be allowed to keep the watch the Nevada legislature had given him, but it went with the loot. So did all his other belongings. Completely believing it was an authentic holdup, he was actually terrified, as he usually was whenever a loaded gun was around. He kept his hands up long after the bandits left, as they had ordered him to do.

When Mark reached Virginia City, he told his friends about the mishap, borrowed a hundred dollars, and bought them a dinner. He even agreed to appear again and use the robbery for a subject. Tickets for the lecture soon were selling at five dollars apiece.

Then one of the gang got drunk and let the cat out of the bag. Mark was furious at being the victim of another practical joke. He researched the law, found that the pranksters could get a stiff sentence, and swore he would prosecute them. They now were the anxious ones. They pleaded with Mark, and returned all the booty, but Mark was adamant.

Only after the stagecoach carrying him to his next engagement was under way, did he put his head out its window and forgive the thieves.

The tour ended in San Francisco in early December, 1866. Mark Twain resolved at last to go back home. He was reasonably rich now, and he was a well-known writer and lecturer. He arranged with McComb for the *Alta California* to buy the travel letters he would send on a proposed future trip around the world, and set sail for the east coast aboard the *America* on December 15.

The captain of the *America* was Ned Wakeman, one of the most colorful seamen of his day. He was a huge man, equally tender and violent, who had been born at sea and had been everywhere, except to school. Nevertheless, he had picked up an enormous amount of information. A religious man, he knew the Bible by heart and had an explanation for all the miracles in it. Mark Twain adored him.

It was a fearful trip and ended with an outbreak of cholera on the ship Mark took from the east coast of Nicaragua, after crossing the Isthmus. He did not reach New York until January 12, 1867.

There, due to the corruption of Mayor Oakey Hall and Boss Tweed, prices were sky-high. Mark stayed just long enough to arrange for the publication in book form of his California sketches, with the jumping frog story as the title one. Then he went to visit old friends, and his mother in St. Louis.

In that city he saw a prospectus of what was to be probably the first "cruise"—an excursion to the Mediterranean countries and the Holy Land aboard a luxury ship, the *Quaker City*. Prominent persons were advertised as having already subscribed as passengers. Mark Twain decided to be one of these, and reserved passage. Then he wrote the *Alta* for the fare—$1,250. McComb persuaded the management that it was a worthwhile investment, and sent the check.

"Your only instructions," the *Alta* manager wrote Mark, "are that you will continue to write at such times and from such places as you deem proper, and in the same style that heretofore secured you the favor of the readers of the *Alta California*." Mark was to be paid twenty dollars a letter.

When Mark Twain went to New York to pick up his ticket, he found his name also advertising the distinguished-passenger list.

The *Quaker City* was not to sail until June, and it was then only April. Mark waited in New York to see his first book through the press. Meanwhile, Frank Fuller, former Acting Governor of Utah, who had known Mark when they were both in the West, insisted that Mark Twain give a lecture in New York. Fuller was to assume all the expenses.

In spite of Mark's timid reluctance, Fuller engaged Cooper Union, then the city's largest auditorium, and advertised the lecture for May 6, 1867, just after Mark's book would have been published. James Nye, now United States Senator from Nevada, was to introduce Mark.

Blasé New York, especially at that time of hot political issues, and with plenty of other attractions, did not quiver with anticipation of a lecture on the Sandwich Islands as Virginia City had. To be sure of an audience, Fuller had to paper the house by sending free tickets to all the schoolteachers in the region.

The hall was jammed. Since Nye had not shown up, Mark himself opened the entertainment with some choice remarks about the absent chairman that got the Westerners in the audience roaring with laughter. Soon the whole audience had caught the infection. Later, Fuller recalled that "people were positively ill for days, laughing at that lecture."

The New York Times reported: "Judging from the success achieved by the lecturer last evening, he should repeat his experiment at an early date." Mark Twain had made it in the big time. Never again would he have to worry about having an empty house.

Now that he was well known, he found New Yorkers more sociable than he had fourteen years before. But he was not used to the apathy of a large city. He made the mistake, for example, of interfering in a street fight, and for his pains got locked up for a night with the scum of New York. He was horrified by the high prices. He was shocked at the daringly diaphanous dress of the chorines in *The Black Crook,* the musical-comedy hit of the day. He was still a country boy, fascinated yet baffled by the ways of a jaded society. It was all startlingly different from the naïvely vigorous, hustling West. In his last New York letter to the *Alta,* Mark confessed that he had "had enough of sights and shows, and noise and bustle, and confusion, and now I want to disperse. I am ready to go."

The *Quaker City,* a side-wheeler with auxiliary sails, steamed out of New York Harbor with sixty-seven passengers. Most of them were older than Mark, and a good many were of the clergy. This factor at first discouraged him, especially as the advertised subscribers had canceled their reservations. But there were also a few young persons whom he found pleasant. During the five-month "picnic," as he described it, he associated mostly with them.

To Americans then, travel beyond the ocean for any purpose other than urgent business was a new thing. Not only was it uncomfortable, expensive, and hazardous, but it held small interest for them. They were intent on building their own world and surviving in it. And they had been stung by visitors from abroad who had not hesitated to point out that the American way of life was hopelessly crude, vulgar, and immature.

The effects of the Civil War changed this pattern. That conflict reinforced the faith of Americans that they had something worth fighting for and preserving. It also won them respect overseas. America was appearing to Europeans no longer as a puzzling, oversized child, but mature, knowing its identity and where it was going.

The result was a sense of ambivalent self-confidence on the part of Americans. On the one hand, they still believed their own way superior to the traditions they had rejected like rebellious children. On the other hand, they suspected that not everything in the Old World was bad. Perhaps they might be in need of the refining influence of a civilization wise because of age and experience. They were emerging from adolescence to find that the old folks were not such fools after all.

The Civil War was being followed by an increase of wealth and leisure, particularly in the East. Those who benefited from it wanted to put it to as broad a use as possible. Travel became popular. Books extolling the glories of Europe were no longer enough; Americans wanted to see for themselves. Only after they had been shown the originals could they know what of their own was adequate and what could stand improvement or replacement.

When Mark Twain's letters about his trip appeared, they were immediately popular, not only because of the vigor and humor of the writing, but also because Mark Twain was seeing the Old World from these new points of view.

Consequently he failed to see on their own terms and in their own context the places he visited. Many things he observed so superficially and so provincially that his reportage is sophomoric and sometimes in bad taste. He could not, for example, perceive the meaning of relics for those who venerate them, and he was cynical about the Catholic faith. He laughed at legends, and he ridiculed the painting of the masters for representing implausibilities. He seemed to expect everything to conform to his preconceived ideas of it or to what he thought it ought to be. When it did not, he tried to annihilate it with a barb, as if unwilling to admit it challenged him. He reported realistically, including the squalor along with the glamour. He was every loyal American abroad for the first time, and he was writing in a way he knew would please his equally innocent countrymen.

He himself was more impressed and instructed than he wished to let on, as certain passages in the letters unintentionally reveal. He found the splendid monuments even more wondrous than he had expected them to be. He felt the spell of antiquity, and was awed by the timelessness of those works of man that had seen generation after generation pass and be forgotten.

By walking where they had stepped, he sensed a closeness to the few mortals who have survived oblivion. He could understand why things had happened as they had, why men had thought as they had, why time and space are the indispensable dimensions of life—all from learning the total context in which kingdoms rise and wane. Through the facile wit, the easy mockery, the immature humor of the letters shines the sensitive spirit that the trip had quickened. Mark Twain returned a broader and a deeper person, generally in love with all he had seen.

He was particularly in love with one tiny item, the velvet-framed miniature portrait of Olivia Langdon, sister of the gay eighteen-year-old Charles who was one of his fellow excursionists. "From that day to this," Mark Twain wrote many years after he had seen the miniature, "she has never been out of my mind." Charley agreed to introduce them, and Mark resolved to remind him of the promise as soon as they reached America.

The meeting was to be postponed. The day after the *Quaker City* docked, Mark was off to Washington. He had been offered a position as secretary to Senator William M. Stewart, whom he had known in his Carson City days. He needed the money; he wanted to get Orion a government job; he had to complete the travel letters he had promised the *Alta California* and the New York *Herald.* He had also been solicited for contributions by many other newspapers and magazines, for the letters which had appeared, as well as his previous work, made him an author much in demand.

It was a dreary winter. Mark hated his job, and he took a dim view of the political maneuverings in the capital. "It could probably be shown by facts and figures," he wrote, "that there is no distinctly native American criminal class except Congress." The confusion of Andrew Johnson's administration was complete. Thanks to his job, Mark Twain could see it from the inside. It was not long before he and Senator Stewart quarreled, and Mark resigned.

He had failed to get Orion a job, but he had had plenty of offers for himself. Socially, too, he had been a success. At a dinner of the Washington Correspondents Club he had delivered a witty, slightly risqué speech on women, and it had brought him praise and notoriety. And he was sending good copy on the Washington scene to papers all over the country. Still, he could not wait to get away from that hateful environment. He was an idealist yet, and he could not take seriously the nonsense of bureaucracy and the pious hypocrisy of the legislators.

The dismal Washington period had one bright interlude. Mark went to New York to spend Christmas with Dan Slote, his *Quaker City* cabin mate. Slote also invited some other of the young "Innocents," including Charley Langdon. Charley asked Mark to dine with him and his family at their hotel.

There Mark saw for the first time the girl whose portrait had so enthralled him in the harbor of Smyrna the previous September. He was not disappointed. She was dazed. He spent New Year's Day at her open house, and she gave him permission to write to her, and offered him an invitation to visit her.

Then he had to go back to Washington. Release came soon. A Hartford, Connecticut, publisher, Elisha Bliss, offered to publish a book based on Mark's *Quaker City* travel letters and promised him a good sale through Bliss's subscription firm, the American Publishing Company. Mark agreed, and went to Hartford to settle the matter.

Then it appeared that the *Alta* had taken out copyright on the letters. Mark sailed for San Francisco to get them released for book publication. From the western coast of Nicaragua he took a ship commanded by his old skipper, Captain Ned Wakeman. During the voyage the captain told Mark the dream that became the basis for *Captain Stormfield's Visit to Heaven.*

Once the *Alta* business was satisfactorily concluded, Mark decided on a lecture tour over the same route as nearly three years before. It was late July before he returned to the East. At once he set out for the Langdon home in Elmira, New York.

7

THE TAMING OF A LION

Jervis Langdon was a self-made man who wanted his four children to have all the advantages he had lacked before he made a fortune in coal mines and coal yards. His favorite of these children was Olivia Louise, called Livy. She was ten years younger than Mark Twain, and had recently been cured by a "faith healer" of injuries sustained six years before from a fall on the ice. Still frail —she would never have robust health—she was a little terrified of the rough, bold, handsome Westerner who was in love with her.

Mark stayed with the Langdons in their huge Elmira house for two weeks, entertaining the whole family, including Jervis Langdon, who had liked him from their first meeting at the St. Nicholas Hotel, on lower Broadway in New York, the previous December. Then Mark popped the question. Livy turned him down. She had to refuse him at least once; she was a shining example of the genteel repression of that era which required a refined young lady to seem not too eager.

Mark had to leave, anyway. As he was being driven to

the train, however, the carriage seat came loose and threw him to the ground. Pretending to be hurt more than he was, he got several days' nursing—and companionship—from Livy. By the time he finally got away, both of them knew that his next proposal, to be made after a proper interval, would be accepted.

He went to Hartford to work with Elisha Bliss on the book of travel letters that would be *The Innocents Abroad.*

Hartford charmed him. It was then a city of about forty thousand persons, with handsome streets and houses. Mark noted its famous industries and its prosperity. To him it represented the dignity, tradition, and intelligent elegance of an old society. Its literary life had begun in the seventeenth century and still continued.

Through Bliss, Mark met the Reverend Joseph H. Twichell, who was to be a lifelong friend. The Blisses also introduced him to the leaders of Hartford's intellectual society, John and Isabella Beecher Hooker, and he stayed a few days at their house.

"I desire to have the respect of this sterling old Puritan community," he wrote a friend, "for their respect is well worth having."

Even though, as the letter continued, he did not "dare smoke after going to bed or do *anything* that's comfortable and natural," he wanted what Hartford had to offer. He believed that he could become a rich man—rich enough to afford to marry Olivia Langdon, rich enough to afford the respectable security of Hartford, Connecticut. To get these advantages became his immediate goal.

He therefore resolved to go on to Boston to sign the contract for lecturing offered him by James Redpath, of the Boston Lyceum Bureau, the leading lecture agent in the country.

Redpath's system distributed lecturers in groups of six or eight to the managers of local lecture series (lyceums).

In each group was one house-filler to every three house-emptiers. The local manager had to take them all. Among Redpath's house-fillers were Henry Ward Beecher, the most famous minister of the time; Horace Greeley, the country's most prominent newspaper editor, whose "Go West, young man!" has become proverbial; Wendell Phillips, the fiery abolitionist; Josh Billings, the popular humorist; Louis Agassiz, the nation's leading naturalist; and Mark Twain. Among the house-emptiers was one Olive Logan, a complete nonentity, whose brief celebrity was due entirely to her husband's promotion of her name, which became a household word for fatuous opinions on anything and everything. Each lecturer appeared about one hundred and ten nights a season for an average fee of $100 an engagement; Redpath got a 10 per cent commission.

On his first tour for Redpath, Mark Twain introduced himself in the words of an embarrassed miner in California who had been unwillingly pressed into service as chairman during Mark's previous tour: "I don't know anything about this man. At least, I know only two things: one is, he hasn't been in the penitentiary, and the other is —I don't know why."

Mark's lectures on his *Quaker City* voyage were so successful that he was often mobbed by his admiring audiences, and people would line up on the streets to watch him pass. He loved the attention and the recognition, but he hated the effort, and wrote his mother that he was afraid he might never get out of the lecture field. There was enough of the old Sam Clemens in him to cause him to write in his notebook: "Fame is a vapor, popularity an accident; the only earthly certainty, oblivion." Still, he could go back to Elmira with over $8,000 in his pocket.

Livy helped him read the proofs of his book. His love for her was increased by his recognition that she could give him the refinement Anson Burlingame had told him he should get. The stability of the Langdon household and the security Livy's pruning of his vulgarity gave him made him feel that perhaps he had at last come home. He need no longer be an outcast and a wanderer; he could be supreme in his own castle, from which there would be no rejection. His warm love of life and of the world was being reflected in Livy's response to him. She accepted his second proposal.

The whole Langdon family by now had accepted him. Jervis Langdon, however, felt obliged to insist that Mark procure character references. Mark Twain might be a famous name and its bearer might be a disarming person; but to the Langdons, none too secure in their own newly acquired wealth and social position, he was only an ex-typesetter, ex-pilot, ex-miner, ex-journalist. None of these occupations was highly regarded. None promised any reliability for the delicate Livy.

Mark's only sources for these references were in the West. He wrote to them. Then, while waiting for the slow mails to bring replies, he went lecturing again.

When Mark returned to Elmira in late January, 1869, Jervis Langdon showed him the letters. One of Mark's friends had written: "Clemens is a humbug." Another prophesied that Mark "would fill a pauper's grave." All agreed that he would make about the worst husband on record.

Mark looked very woebegone.

Jervis Langdon held out his hand. "Take the girl," he said. "I know you better than they do."

Mark's engagement to Livy was announced a few days later, on February 4, 1869.

It would not have been proper for them to be married at once. A long engagement was considered obligatory for a girl of Olivia Langdon's social position. Besides, Mark

Twain needed a regular income. He wanted a job near enough to Elmira so that Livy would not be homesick for her family, on whom she was emotionally dependent.

He found that these conditions would be satisfied if he could afford to buy a third interest in the Buffalo, New York, *Express*. To raise the money, he again went lecturing, this time with another famous humorist, Petroleum Vesuvius Nasby (David Ross Locke). Nasby would begin his lecture by announcing: "We are all descended from grandfathers," a statement which became a popular byword.

The tour was even more successful than Mark's previous one, because *The Innocents Abroad* had been published and was a best seller. Reviews of it in the East were reserved, however, except for that of William Dean Howells in the *Atlantic Monthly*, which led to a close friendship between Twain and Howells.

By August, 1869, Mark Twain had taken up his duties on the *Express*, Jervis Langdon having loaned him half of the $25,000 purchase price. The *Express* had been a dull, farmers' paper. Mark worked hard to enliven it. His contributions may have gratified the elementary sense of humor of the subscribers, but they seem wan when read today. He joked about his engagement in banal terms, sharply criticized the obvious mismanagement of the departing President Andrew Johnson, ridiculed Susan B. Anthony's campaign for women's rights, denounced the monopolistic enterprises of Commodore Vanderbilt, kept alive the misunderstandings Harriet Beecher Stowe had started about Lord Byron, and wrote parodies of the sentimental novels of the day. It was all a flogging of several dead horses.

The humor is either vulgar—jokes about boardinghouse keepers' false hair getting into the hash; or cruel—ridicule of old maids; or ghastly puns—"Cotton is no longer king; in the late war it was worsted"; or anecdotes of the following variety:

Grocer (to "African gentleman"): Don't you want any of that ham?

African gentleman (who has smelled ham in question): Well, no, boss. De sign reads "sugar-cured hams." Dat 'ar' ham's sick yet. My advice to you is to change the medicine.

Clearly Mark Twain's mind was on his fiancée. His work for the *Express* was forgotten for many years, and should remain so.

The lovers were married on February 2, 1870. Officiating at the ceremony were the Reverend Thomas K. Beecher, brother of Henry Ward Beecher, and the Langdons' liberal Presbyterian minister; and the Reverend Joseph H. Twichell who, with his wife Harmony, had come from Hartford to Elmira for the occasion.

Mark had planned to live modestly in a Buffalo boardinghouse until he was out of debt for the purchase of the *Express*. His new father-in-law had had other plans. The couple were escorted by the wedding party to fashionable Delaware Avenue, where Jervis Langdon had bought them a splendid house, completely furnished in the blue-and-white Eastlake style, then the height of fashion. He had also staffed it with servants.

Mark had finally seen the last of the boardinghouses he had detested since he was fifteen years old. But he now had to get used to home life and to a sweetheart who had become a wife. Mark always adored his Livy, but the marriage was not a perfect one for a man of Mark Twain's personality and genius.

One fault was Mark's lack of experience with women. He had never had anything more than a flirtation with a girl, and had never known a woman intimately. His ignorance of a woman's nature and feelings was due partly to his having lived in an almost exclusively masculine environment, but more to his regarding young women not so much as human beings as unearthly angels. This was particularly true if the girl was one of breeding and refinement. The middle-aged and older women of provincial Missouri and the wilderness he seemed to appreciate. He could vividly create a motherly Aunt Polly or Aunt Sally, or a Mrs. Judith Loftus. Roxy, the near-white slave mother in *Pudd'nhead Wilson,* is a dynamic figure, motivated by devotion to her worthless son. But his fictional heroines, like Laura Hawkins in *The Gilded Age,* are unbelievable; and he wrote of Joan of Arc as if she were a wax doll.

Olivia Langdon Clemens appears to have been a colorless, none too courageous, utterly conventional woman. Too overbred to show passion, she probably felt none. She was not unintelligent, however. Most of the vulgarities and improprieties she pruned out of Mark Twain's literary style made for an improvement. If she curtailed his exuberance, it was because he believed he should let her tame him. It was a hard process for both of them.

Mark's conduct often embarrassed Livy, and she let him know it. Her rebukes and reproaches hurt him, for he idolized her as she was, whereas she was trying to alter him. Mark Twain's "In Defense of Harriet Shelley" shows, by his protesting too much, that he thought every man owed devotion and fidelity to his wife, regardless of her character. He did not choose to accept the fact that Harriet was a nitwit and that therefore Shelley, a genius, could not live with her. The ways of genius are as uncommon as geniuses themselves. By submitting to the domination of Livy's unimaginative respectability, Mark Twain probably reduced his own capacities. The inability of either to surmount the griefs that befell them suggests that their feelings for each other were not strong enough to sustain them.

From the time of his marriage onward, the conflict

between Samuel Clemens and Mark Twain became harder to reconcile. The rejected youth—ironically, Livy's nickname for him was Youth—would be subtly rejected by the woman he had chosen to represent home and mother to him.

Their first years together were marred by unfortunate events. Jervis Langdon died, and so did a dear friend of Livy's who was visiting them. Livy's first child, a boy they named Langdon, was born prematurely, and Livy's fragile health suffered from the experience.

Mark decided to give up the Buffalo house, now full of unhappy memories. He saw the importance of producing more and more books as a source of income and as a hedge against oblivion, and he recognized the advisability of being near his publisher, Elisha Bliss.

Bliss was not one to let his profitable author rest content with lecturing. He demonstrated to Mark that the success of *The Innocents Abroad* was due to the presence in it of the Mark Twain personality. There lay the same humor that filled the lecture halls. In a book it would be permanent, for man makes nothing so hard to destroy as a book.

Mark was convinced that his future lay in books. He could see that the pieces he was contributing to the *Express*, and to the *Galaxy*, a New York magazine that paid him well for a humorous monthly column, were ephemeral. Moreover, they were reaching too small a readership, whereas *The Innocents Abroad* was being read and loved all over America. He knew he could write for the great public he understood, and that it responded enthusiastically.

Mark needed a large income to keep up the expensive establishment he thought part of his responsibility to Livy. Actually, she was more economical than he, since she had been longer used to money. Thanks to Bliss's method of subscription selling, books were being brought to the people; they did not have to go after them. The system was rather like the modern book club. Bliss promised good sales.

When Bliss proposed a book on Mark's experiences in the West, and offered a contract for it, Mark agreed. From then on, he began to think of himself as a literary personage.

The book was to be delivered to Bliss at the end of 1870. By July 15 of that year, Mark had begun work on what was to be *Roughing It*, a greater book than *The Innocents Abroad* because it dealt with an episode in which he had been deeply involved personally, rather than with such an arbitrary experience as a brief trip abroad. He enjoyed writing it and felt he was writing well, though with too many interruptions. He resolved to dispose of everything that interfered with this new development in his career.

By April, 1871, it was clear that in spite of Mark's efforts, the circulation of the *Express* was not increasing. He sold his interest in it at a loss of $10,000, and also gave up the *Galaxy* column. Then he put up for sale the Buffalo house, which had proved costly to maintain, and went with Livy and little Langdon to Quarry Farm, the home of his brother-in-law Theodore Crane, in the hope that there he could finish the long-overdue book.

It was the first of many summers the Clemenses were to spend at this large, pleasant house on a hill overlooking Elmira and the Chemung Valley. Mark worked all summer on *Roughing It*, greatly encouraged by a visit from Joseph Goodman, his old boss on the Virginia City *Enterprise*, who read the manuscript and praised it.

That autumn, Mark moved his family to Hartford, where he leased the house of John and Isabella Hooker in Nook Farm, about three miles from the center of the city.

Twenty years before, John Hooker had bought the one-hundred-acre tract, and then had sold parts of it to a group of intellectuals carefully selected by him and his wife. Hooker was a descendant of the founder of Hartford; his wife, a sister of Henry Ward Beecher, was an ardent feminist. Besides this strong-minded couple the principals of the group were Charles Dudley Warner, part owner and editor of the Hartford *Courant;* Harriet Beecher Stowe, Isabella Hooker's sister and the author of *Uncle Tom's Cabin;* Joseph Twichell; and now Mark Twain.

They were all close friends. "Each of us," wrote Hooker, "made free of the others' houses . . . each keeping open house, and all of us frequently gathering for a social evening or to welcome some friendly visitor, often some person distinguished in political, literary or philanthropic life who had come to some of our houses."

They provided an element of intellectual stimulation Mark had missed in Buffalo. They were also thrifty New Englanders, and wrote for money. Mark quickly realized how great their importance would be to him now that he was embarked on a literary career. Talent rarely thrives in a desert.

Almost as quickly he perceived what the personal cost of this new life would be to him. He knew he would have to conform, and he thought he wanted to, but he did not completely understand all the conventions of this intelligent but provincial group, with their highly developed moral sense.

This amounted to strict observance of a code to which they believed the world should subscribe. They did not like the world as they found it. The abstractions of truth, goodness, and piety were the weapons of the spiritual tyranny they inflicted on themselves and on others. They allowed no compromise.

Mark Twain had seen too much of life to be that rigid.

The source of his humor was his appreciation of humanity, his admiration and love of human beings who followed their own nature and were neither better nor worse for their individuality. If he found man considerably lower than the angels, he also found him a creature of life and love, and noble in his survival of the tricks God plays on him. He would not believe in a principle that did not serve human needs.

To him a lie was not a lie and a sin, when it could save a soul. He thought swearing a natural and necessary release of tension, not the breaking of a Commandment. He thought it immoral to impose impossible ideals on real human beings, and believed such a course would lead to hypocrisy. He had learned to live in the world and cope with it on its own terms. He enjoyed its infinite variety, even its confusion. He felt no need to subdue it to his own standards for the sake of weeping over its failure to meet them.

This conflict of attitudes produced strong tensions in him. His new friends liked him as a person in spite of what they thought his eccentricity, and thus they showed that they, too, had a sense of humor. He liked these idealists and reformers, regardless of their high moral tone, but he found it hard to swallow their eternal moralizing.

Moralizing was a favorite spiritual diversion in those days of the genteel tradition. The more a person could moralize—that is, adjust the world to his code—the more virtuous he appeared and the more he was respected by other moralizers. Moralizing somehow managed to equate rank in the social order with status among God's elect. It symbolized the degeneracy of the old Puritan concept of grace apparent through behavior.

Charles Dudley Warner, for example, could write that the value of a kitchen garden is not so much to produce vegetables as it is to teach "the higher virtues. . . . The garden thus becomes a moral agent, as it was in the beginning." He gave each of the vegetables a moral value, and consequently a social one: "The cucumber is a low comedian in the company where the melon is a minor gentleman."

To Mark Twain, whom the Boston critics had as good as called a "low comedian" but who desperately wanted to become a "minor gentleman," moralizing was an irritating private reminder that he was different from the Nook Farm group. Livy herself "belonged"; she was an incurable moralizer.

She also followed the Bible to the letter. Mark, who knew the Bible quite as well as she, maintained that he could not believe in the God he saw depicted in it—a Being more cruel than kind, as well as inconsistent and illogical. Mark Twain was not then, nor did he ever seem to become, familiar with the new higher criticism that, as a result of discoveries about the physical nature of the universe, regarded much of the Bible more as myth than as fact. He asked Livy not to urge him to take the Bible, as he found it, for a spiritual guide.

Shortly after his marriage, these restrictions on the free belief he had been developing since his first wanderings began to create a tension he released by composing the "Papers of the Adam Family." These pretended to be translations by the "Father of History" of the diaries of Adam, Eve, Methuselah, and other ancients. They are, of course, burlesques of the myths of Genesis. A few were eventually published, but they so offended Livy that the majority, which show Mark's greatest disgust, remained in his private papers until after his death. They were rumblings of the violent and bitter explosions of his later years.

A great help to Mark Twain in resolving these philosophical problems was Joseph Twichell. Twichell was solidly one of the group; he was also a somewhat freer spirit, with as great a love for the earthiness and perversity of man as Mark's own. Together, Twichell and Mark took long walks during which they discussed this conflict, to the relief of both. It was for Twichell that Mark Twain later wrote *1601*, an imaginary conversation in the court of Queen Elizabeth I on topics and in language that would have brought them instant expulsion from the scrupulously landscaped Eden of Nook Farm.

From time to time Mark escaped from this manicured respectability to the less rarefied atmosphere of his fellow lecturers on the Redpath circuit. They would spend their days at Young's Hotel in Boston, then in the evenings go to the nearby small towns to try out their new lectures before tackling the more critical audience of the cities. They spent many hours together, smoking, trading experiences, swapping stories, and talking shop.

Among them was Josh Billings (Henry W. Shaw), the successor to Artemus Ward as America's most popular humorist. Mark and Billings became close friends. Billings is now almost forgotten, except for the fact that any boy with that surname is inevitably nicknamed "Josh." Possibly his most famous line was: "The difficulty is not that we know so much, but that we know so much that isn't so."

Billings, in the massacred English that amused readers then, described the difficulties of preparing for a visit from Mark Twain.

> *If yu expeckt Mark Twain to be happy, or even kumfortable, you hav got to buy a box of cigars worth at least seventeen dollars and yu hav got to move all the tender things out ov yure parlor. Yu hav got to skatter all the latest papers around the room careless, yu hav got to hav a pitcher ov ice-water handy, for*

Mark is a dry humorist. Yu hav got to ketch and tie all yure yung ones, hed and foot, for Mark luvs babys only in theory; yu hav got to send yure favorite kat over to the nabors and hide yure poodle.

Bret Harte was in Boston then, and frequently joined Mark and his new literary friends: William Dean Howells, the editor of the *Atlantic Monthly;* and Thomas Bailey Aldrich, the editor of *Every Saturday,* who had just published his *Story of a Bad Boy.* The last two were about the only Boston writers and reviewers who then appreciated Mark Twain's originality. The older, academic critics thought him trivial, crude, and worst of all, unclassifiable. They had small appreciation of his uniqueness. Mark Twain's appeal was primarily to the equally warmhearted American public, which was only just beginning to free itself from the esthetic domination of chilly Boston.

Lecturing and the social life of Hartford kept, and were to keep, Mark Twain so busy during the winters that he did little actual writing there. He merely planned what he would complete in the quiet of Quarry Farm, where he built an octagonal study for himself away from the main house. In Hartford also he indulged in less demanding exercises of his imagination than writing. He had already invented and patented an adjustable waistcoat strap; now, in 1872, he produced "The Mark Twain Scrapbook." This invention did away with the messiness of a pastepot by substituting dry mucilage on the pages themselves, which then needed only to be moistened, like an envelope flap, and the items attached. Mark gave the manufacturing rights to Dan Slote's firm, and derived a steady income from them.

In that year Mark's first daughter, Olivia Susan, called Susy, was born. Two and a half months later, Mark took little Langdon for a carriage ride and absentmindedly forgot to keep the child warmly covered. The two-year-old caught a heavy cold, and died. Mark blamed himself painfully, sensing his old guilt over similar disasters which seemed to come from his unconscious unwillingness to cope with the details of responsibility. Livy took the death of Langdon even more heavily. To recover his spirits, Mark went to England, leaving Livy to console herself with the new baby.

The Innocents Abroad had just been published in London. When Mark arrived there, he found himself almost as celebrated as he was in his own country. Leading authors and journalists came to call on him and entertained him. Banquets were given for him, and his skill as an afterdinner speaker made the British realize that Mark Twain was a personality they could not match. They loved him and begged him to return.

When reports on his reception in England reached America, institutions thought it should be imitated at home. Mark was elected to membership in New York's Lotos Club, one of the city's associations of men of talent. He was invited to speak at more banquets and other gatherings than he could possibly attend.

The year 1873 saw the Clemenses very much a part of the Hartford group. Mark bought land in Nook Farm, and commissioned the architect Edward Tuckerman Potter to build him a house that would represent his new status and social ambitions. If he could appear as a substantial man of property, perhaps his spiritual reservations might be overlooked. It seemed worth the enormous cost, even if he would have to keep on the hated lecture circuit to pay for it.

At a dinner party that winter the women complained of the stupidity of the novels they had been reading. They challenged their husbands to write better ones. Mark Twain and Charles Dudley Warner declared they would do one together. Mark had an idea for a novel, but he was diffident about undertaking such an extended piece of fiction alone.

Warner welcomed the chance of linking his name with that of Mark Twain. *The Innocents Abroad* and *Roughing It,* which had been published in 1872, were best sellers. Warner had written several books of travel, collections of essays, and a biography or two, and was in demand as an editor. He was quite unskilled in the art of storytelling, however, and had little experience in creating character.

The subject they chose was political corruption in contemporary America, with a theme of public loss for private gain. Each wrote approximately the same number of chapters. The result, *The Gilded Age,* is a jumble of styles, attitudes, plots and subplots, and unmotivated actions.

The better parts are those Mark Twain contributed, for at least he had firsthand experience with the way government in Washington was run. The only character who comes alive and is at all memorable is Mark's Colonel Sellers, the incurable optimist and visionary, whose dreams wreck everyone's fortunes, but whose generous nature makes up for it. Sellers, modeled after Mark's cousin James Lampton, has some of Mark Twain in him, too. Like the indomitable Colonel, Mark had seen America as a land where "the paths to fortune are innumerable and all open" and where there is "invitation in the air and success in the wide horizon."

The title has become synonymous with the greed of the Reconstruction period in American history, but the novel criticizes the system of an expansionist economy less than it does the uncouth people involved in it. They are simply not nice Nook Farm gentry.

Once the novel was finished, Mark and his family sailed for England, to wait out the completion of their own house in Hartford. They were gone six months, during which Mark was as warmly received as on his previous visit. They returned in January, 1874, to find *The Gilded Age*, published the previous December, selling well.

Mark needed the money; the house was not yet finished, and its costs were increasing daily. Hounded by the financial demands of life in Hartford, he went to Elmira in April, determined to write hard. From then on, he was to join the idealistic Nook Farm authors in their unceasing quest of money. Soon after he reached the peace of his Quarry Farm study, he began what would be his first masterpiece.

8

TOM SAWYER IS BORN

Four days after his marriage to Livy, Mark Twain wrote to his boyhood chum Will Bowen a letter including tender reminiscences of their carefree days in Hannibal twenty-odd years before. Mark was ecstatically happy with his bride, his new sense of security, his success. Everything had a rosy glow. If there had been clouds over his childhood, he forgot them. It seemed the one other blissful period in his life.

The image of that glorious morning of youth stayed with him so vividly that it fairly cried out to be expressed. He needed to communicate its joy and beauty. Two years later he tried to recreate it in a play and then in the form of a boy's diary. The diary records a puppy-love affair and a few of the incidents of *Tom Sawyer*. The play begins in the same way *Tom Sawyer* does, with a harassed aunt calling for a wayward boy to come home.

Mark Twain abandoned both efforts. Something was lacking in his understanding of his childhood. He could not find a suitable symbol to express all his feeling—only the rapturous sense of being young and free and amusingly naïve. There was nothing to contrast with this devotion, no conflict to give it variety and life.

In the next two years his life changed. Sorrow and responsibility burdened him. He had entered a world full of restrictions, among which he felt he must thread his way cautiously as if in a labyrinth. Yet it was an exciting journey, and he was sure there would be treasure at the end of the tortuous passages. With unconscious reluctance the boy he had been had become the man he was. They were, of course, the same person.

The symbol he was seeking now began to emerge into consciousness. The boy he would write about would be a dreamer and a rebel, wending his way through the harrowing difficulties of his world to find a treasure that would redeem him and restore him to the society from which he felt an outcast.

Such is the essential story of Tom Sawyer. It is also the essential story of a major part of Mark Twain's existence. It was, in fact, so close to actuality that Mark Twain found great difficulty in transforming through his imagination the specific into the abstract, the perishable individual into the enduring symbol. For he wanted to write not of himself alone, but of his experience as one common to all people. Only by seeing it as not unique and therefore as having meaning could he resolve his own problems.

There were practical considerations as well. He was timid and anxious. He had never written a novel alone; never before had he needed to *transform* an experience, instead of merely *record* one. The novel would have to be a success, too; otherwise he might lose the public he had gained. Even *The Gilded Age* was going into its third edition in one year. Still, the story had to be told.

He recalled that his friend Thomas Bailey Aldrich's recollections of his own childhood in *The Story of a Bad Boy* had been well received. It seemed as if the adults of their time enjoyed freeing themselves from the iron chains of respectability by seeing the days of youth as golden ones. But Aldrich's story, charming though it was, did not get off the ground. His "bad boy" was just one boy, and the story was only a nostalgic narrative that fulfilled no dream. Perhaps, Mark thought, he could surpass the model and still gratify the same trend in the public's taste.

All through the summer of 1874 he worked hard at Quarry Farm on the manuscript of what was to be *The Adventures of Tom Sawyer*. Then the problem of transforming his experiences blocked him. His "inspiration tank," as he put it, ran dry.

He returned to Hartford and dramatized the chapters and characters he had contributed to *The Gilded Age*. The play was called *Colonel Sellers* after the unforgettable character Mark Twain had forged out of his cousin and, unconsciously, out of himself. Colonel Sellers is the tempter luring the homeless Hawkins family (John Marshall and Orion Clemens) into the wilderness with his schemes to make a fortune. The theme, though treated as farce, is not far from that of *Tom Sawyer*.

The dramatization, somewhat adapted to his own talents by the actor John T. Raymond, who impersonated the Colonel, ran for nearly two years. Mark Twain's share of the profits was over one hundred thousand dollars.

Mark later wrote in his *Autobiography* that he was not satisfied with Raymond's portrayal of Colonel Sellers. He felt that Raymond had exaggerated the character, whom Mark had "put on paper as he was," and had thus reduced the Colonel in stature. But Raymond had done with Colonel Sellers just what Mark Twain was struggling to do with Tom Sawyer: namely, to abstract himself into a universal character by omitting the particulars which belonged only to the individual. Although he did not acknowledge it in the *Autobiography*, Mark Twain had got from Raymond a lesson in abstracting. Raymond, an outsider, could universalize the fictitious Sellers, whom Mark Twain could see only as a real, individual man, part of whom was himself. What Mark had to do was get outside Tom Sawyer, who was also himself. Raymond's success in the play bolstered Mark Twain's confidence.

In the spring of 1874, William Dean Howells and Thomas Bailey Aldrich had visited Mark Twain in Hartford. Howells described Mark as smoking continuously and "soothing his tense nerves with a mild hot Scotch while they talked and talked and talked." Mark sometimes would tell of his early life, which Howells said was "the inexhaustible, the fairy, the *Arabian Nights* story, which I could never tire of even when it began to be told over again."

In the autumn, Howells visited Mark again in his newly completed house. Howells needed material for the *Atlantic Monthly.* Remembering his enchantment at Mark's tales of a Missouri boyhood, Howells urged him to write them up for the magazine. Mark hesitated, but Joseph Twichell, after hearing the same stories during one of their walks, convinced Mark that he should gratify Howells.

But Mark Twain had not yet mastered the transformation of his childhood. Instead, he began sending to the *Atlantic* stories of his days as a river pilot. In writing these, he encountered no block in expressing his personal frustrations and desires. They could be pure narrative, with a minimum of subjective interpretation. Work on them refilled his inspiration tank. He returned to *Tom Sawyer* and wrote steadily until it was finished in early July, 1875.

He was so nervous about this first novel, which was so intimate a part of him, that he took it to Boston himself to entreat Howells' opinion as soon as possible. A few days later, Howells wrote that he had stayed up until one in the morning to finish the manuscript. Howells added: "It is altogether the best boy story I ever read. It will be an immense success."

His judgment was heartily endorsed by the public when the book was published in December, 1876—and it has been endorsed ever since.

Tom Sawyer is a "boy story," but it is not a boy's story, though boys have loved it. What boy would not wish to do the things Tom does: hoodwinking his friends into getting his chores done for him; winning a prize by a shrewd trick; saving his sweetheart by a noble lie; holding the final clue to a murder; finding a buried treasure? There is a continuous and mounting thrill in the novel; Tom is scared to death most of the time he is involved in his adventures, and they get more and more perilous. His life is in danger, but so is his soul; and he worries as much about the one as about the other. He has too much conscience to torture those he thinks abuse him, but who he knows love him and whom he himself loves. His return from pirating to tell his Aunt Polly that he is really safe is as touching and true a picture of a boy's confused feelings as was ever made. Tom fulfills every lively boy's dream of what he would like to do and be. Few young readers can fail to identify with Tom.

This is the great fun, the enduring humor of the book. As young readers grow older, they can still appreciate this charm, but they can also see what Howells immediately perceived: that is, that *Tom Sawyer* has the quality of a great poem. It is, as Mark Twain said, "a hymn put into prose to give it a worldly air." The hymn celebrates the paradise of youth with all the joys and glories that come from longing for a distant land, vanished but not forgotten. It suggests far more than it says. The names of the characters and places are simply the vocabulary of the universal language of feelings. It rises from this level of a concrete, plausible story to a higher level. Here are the abstractions of steadfastness, loyalty, fear, love, self-preservation, and self-destruction. Still higher is the level of understanding of life in its picture of the exile seeking a home.

The very facts that Tom Sawyer's age is never stated and that an incredible number of events take place within a single, vaguely dated summer are enough to give *Tom Sawyer* the quality every great novel has—a picture of life itself suspended in time and creating an atmosphere of its own within its frame.

Tom Sawyer at last communicated what Mark Twain long had felt. It is a novel about rebellion. It deals with escape from restrictive situations into a position from which these can be surmounted and controlled. Its motivations are the desire for revenge on the cruel, unfeeling world; for fair and generous treatment, and apologies for injustice. It responds to the universal dream of freedom and justification.

It is also a novel about outcasts. Tom Sawyer is an orphan. His mother is dead. There is no mention of his father, or of the nature of either parent. Mark Twain is revealing that when he was a child, his own family were strangers to him. Mark's brother Henry, whose death he unconsciously wished, becomes a detestable half brother ostensibly more appreciated than Tom. Mark felt too different from his gentle-natured sister to represent her as more than a cousin. Mark's mother, whose harsh treatment of him he did not understand, is called an aunt, though she keeps her own character. The implication is that no real mother could be so unjust as Tom's Aunt Polly seemed to the boy who, nevertheless, loved and pitied her.

Huckleberry Finn is an extension of Mark Twain—what he would have liked to be. Hence, in the novel, Huck appears as Tom's other self. He is the realist foil to the dreamer hero. Huck, too, is motherless—the son of the town pariah. He is the true outcast. Tom's father is non-existent, but Huck's is an enemy. Huck's desires are the same as Tom's, but when they are realized and Huck is accepted into society, he rebels, whereas Tom is content. Huck must return to his easy, unrestricted way of life. Still he is not morally irresponsible; he has risked his life to save another's, and he makes clearer distinctions between right and wrong than the more sophisticated Tom. Huck is the fulfillment of another universal dream—that the best life is the life of nature.

Because Huck and Tom are projections of Mark Twain himself, his feeling about them and their whole environment is direct and sure—a genuine love. This emotional certainty brings the book alive, just as the conflict in each of the two boys, who are really one, makes it forceful. The beauty of childhood shines through it, unblemished by the mocking burlesque which blots Mark Twain's other reminiscences, written when he was unsure of his feelings. He was beginning to understand himself, though he was still far from solving the total mystery.

In the winter after *Tom Sawyer* was finished, Mark Twain's turn came to read a paper before Hartford's Monday Evening Club, a gathering of intellectuals that met at the homes of its members. Mark had been elected two years before and had considerably spiced the proceedings with his comments and his papers. These were serious in content, but humorous in style.

For his subject in 1876, Mark chose the conflict he had externalized in *Tom Sawyer*. He was trying to reconcile the narrow Calvinistic training of his youth with the broader attitudes he had acquired through his mature experiences. He was also trying to harmonize the independence necessary to him as an individual with the conformity demanded by society.

The paper, published later that year by Howells in the

Atlantic as "The Facts on the Recent Carnival of Crime in Connecticut," is a story of a man's battle with his conscience. Conscience is personified as an imp that tortures the man much as the bird of evil does Edgar Allan Poe in "The Raven." In fact, that poem and Mark Twain's story have much in common. The man finally kills the imp, which is part of himself. It might even be called his other self, a *doppelgänger.*

The roles of Tom and Huck were being exchanged in Mark Twain's mind. In *Tom Sawyer,* Huck had been Tom's worse self, and a subordinate character. Now Huck was emerging as the truer projection of Mark Twain's personality. Tom, or conscience, was becoming a minor character and something of a nuisance.

Tom Sawyer, "The Carnival of Crime," and *Huckleberry Finn* are Mark Twain's attempts to account for his own duality. He felt that in each person the world sees there is another person—not a slave, but independent, and with a distinct character. The single individual is in reality two beings, a Jekyll-Hyde combination. A man's character is formed by his inborn nature and his modifying conscience working together. Conscience is the other person. But it is not separate, because it has no originality; it is the product of training. "It is," he wrote in his *Notebook,* "whatever one's mother and Bible and comrades and system of government and habitat and heredities have made it." These two persons in a man have no command over each other and are not aware of each other's existence. He was to labor with this dilemma all his life.

Mark Twain's inventions, lectures, and books had made him a rich man, but his expenses kept pace with his earnings. In one year the cost of his lavish style of living in Hartford rose to $100,000. He thoroughly enjoyed the leisure this wealth afforded him, and spent less time on writing. He had quite given up lecturing for money, though he sometimes spoke for the benefit of a charity. For a year or more, only short stories came from his pen—or rather, his typewriter. He had seen one of the first machines in Boston and, fascinated as always by new inventions, had bought one. He copied *Tom Sawyer* on it, and claimed it was the world's first typewritten manuscript.

The stories were being bought by Howells' *Atlantic Monthly* at record prices. Mark was pleased to appear in this leading literary magazine, and loved to be included in the "*Atlantic* dinners" in Boston, along with other celebrated contributors.

He was becoming more of a family man. Red-haired Susy was developing a personality much like his own, and he adored her. Another daughter, Clara, had arrived in 1874. But much as he loved his children, he hated taking the responsibility for them. Once, while wheeling Clara, he absentmindedly let go of the carriage, which careened down the Quarry Farm hill and dumped the baby before he could catch it.

By the summer of 1876 he had begun a continuation of *Tom Sawyer*, which eventually became *The Adventures of Huckleberry Finn*. But he did not like it, and set it aside for several years. For some strange reason he preferred another novel he started but never finished. The manuscript fragment is terrible. He seemed to have lost sight of his dream. Perhaps he thought it had come true in his prosperity. He relapsed into burlesque to disguise his lack of strong feelings about a subject.

He wrote many inferior stories to satisfy the demands of the magazine editors who were beseeching him for material. At the end of the year, Bret Harte came to Hartford, and Mark collaborated with him on a play about a Chinese laundryman. Called *Ah Sin,* it was a miserable failure.

The only productions worthy of Mark Twain at this

period of his life were the articles about his days as a pilot on the Mississippi River. Here again was a lost world he could dream of recapturing, and could recreate in his writing. The passing of that epoch in his life, when he was a king in the pilothouse, triumphing over the relentless, impersonal, deadly Mississippi, had left a sad void in his heart. He filled it now as he relived those years.

The articles had appeared from January to July, 1875, in the *Atlantic Monthly* and had been picked up by many newspapers, as well as pirated in book form. They were called "Old Times on the Mississippi." Elisha Bliss offered Mark a contract for them as a book. To get more material, Mark proposed to Howells a trip down the river, but it was postponed and postponed, and the book was delayed for seven years.

The year 1877 was also unproductive, marked only by another unsuccessful play, *Simon Wheeler, Detective.* It was never produced, and is notable only as showing a new interest of Mark's—the field of detection. He regarded detection as humorous, consisting only of an understanding and acceptance of human beings as they are. The clue to any baffling occurrence could, he thought, be easily found in the vagaries of human nature. There was no need of making a mystery of it. Later he burlesqued the so-called science of detection in *Tom Sawyer, Detective, A Double-Barreled Detective Story,* and "The Stolen White Elephant."

He also began a novel on the theme of mistaken or exchanged identities—a possibility that fascinated him because of the problem of his own personality. His idea originated in his reading of a children's book by the then popular author Charlotte M. Yonge. This told the story of a thirteenth-century English prince who had lived in disguise as a beggar. Mark projected a double exchange of personality—prince as beggar, and beggar as prince—in some colorful period of history. His extensive reading in English history suggested Edward VI, who succeeded his father Henry VIII at the age of nine in 1547. It could be another novel about a young boy.

He attacked the tale enthusiastically, procuring a sizable reference library on the period. Then he encountered plot trouble. His inspiration tank went dry again, and he did not take up the story for two years. It was to be *The Prince and the Pauper*.

At the end of the year, Mark Twain was invited to speak at a contributors' dinner to be given in Boston by the *Atlantic Monthly,* in honor of the seventieth birthday of the saintly poet John Greenleaf Whittier. It was to be attended by Ralph Waldo Emerson, Henry Wadsworth Longfellow, and Oliver Wendell Holmes, New England's most revered and distinguished men of letters. Mark Twain considered it a great honor for him—a newcomer to the ranks of literature, and a Westerner to boot—to be invited.

At the Hotel Brunswick on December 17, 1877, William Dean Howells introduced him to the gathering as one of his dearest friends and "a humorist who never left you hanging your head for having enjoyed his joke."

Mark began a lecture that he had carefully prepared. It described three drunken tramps visiting a cabin in a California mining camp. They identified themselves as Emerson, Longfellow, and Holmes and replied to every remark of their outraged host with an appropriate and familiar quotation from their works. The physical appearance of each of the three was satirized, and they were represented as playing cards all night, drinking, and roistering. Finally they were unmasked as imposters.

After Mark had been speaking for a few minutes, he noticed a deathly, ominous hush in the banquet room. None of the fifty guests was even smiling. Most of them were staring embarrassedly at their plates. Too late he realized that this was not the kind of joke proper Bostonians appreciated. Emerson and Longfellow they regarded as little short of divine, and Holmes was their highly respected doctor and professor, as well as poet. Mark could not stop; he had to go on. When at last he could sit, only one guest was laughing—out of sheer nervousness. No other scheduled speaker dared follow this exhibition.

Mark Twain spent a sleepless night. He returned to Hartford sure that he had ruined himself in Boston forever, and sick with shame over what he had done. He wrote apologies to each of the three "tramps." Emerson was too senile even to have understood the speech, but his daughter answered that she was disappointed when she read the lecture. The others replied good-naturedly.

Actually the speech, though using dialect and some coarse expressions, is witty, and Mark Twain's introduction of the quotations is clever. Anywhere else it would have brought down the house, but the Boston newspapers reported it as the greatest insult their city had received since the British tea tax.

On Mark Twain's part it was a sign of shyness and insecurity. Faced with the "greats" of America, he armed himself with the only weapon he could trust: broad and bluff burlesque. It backfired, wounding him instead of his target. Sadly he realized that the refining process to which he had submitted himself was not complete. Livy's work was not yet done. He resolved to consult her more than ever and to humble himself to her opinions, literary and otherwise.

To get over his embarrassment, Mark Twain took his family to Europe early in 1878. They stayed in Germany until August, when Joseph Twichell joined them at Mark's invitation. The two went on a walking tour of Switzerland.

Then the family spent the autumn in Italy, the winter in Munich, the spring in Paris and London. It was September, 1879, before they returned to Hartford.

The long excursion proved very little. Mark learned more German and was exposed to opera and painting, none of which he liked. Only in his old age did he care for any music but sentimental songs, folk tunes, and Negro spirituals. He liked only extremely representational painting, or the "cheerful chromo."

The tour of Switzerland, however, gave him some good material for the travel book Bliss wanted from him. Bliss published it in March, 1880, as *A Tramp Abroad.* It sold well on the strength of its predecessor, *The Innocents Abroad,* but it is vastly inferior to that classic, which is still a fairly reliable guidebook.

The writing of *A Tramp Abroad* had bored Mark—a good reason for its failure to hold readers today. He was impatient to finish it so that he could go back to *The Prince and the Pauper,* for which his inspiration had revived. He saw now how the original story could be enriched by making it a vehicle for exposing and condemning the harsh laws and cruel punishments that existed in the sixteenth century. It was his way of saying that a refuge in the past, as a glorious period, is an unsafe one.

When it was published, in December, 1881, Mark Twain stood alone as a prominent American author. The earlier flood of literature had subsided. Of its creators—Cooper, Poe, Melville, Hawthorne, Longfellow, Lowell, Whittier, Emerson, Thoreau, Holmes—only a few were still alive, and they were like old electric light bulbs. Howells had not yet produced his fine novels, and Henry James had just begun to attract attention. Having little to choose from, the public gave *The Prince and the Pauper* a warmer reception than it deserved.

Tom Sawyer had puzzled readers accustomed to books

about young people like the innocuous *Story of a Bad Boy*, or Louisa M. Alcott's simpering *Little Men* and others, or the Horatio Alger inspirational hoaxes, or the moralistic "Five Little Peppers" series. Much as the reading public loved the freshness and depth of *Tom Sawyer*, they did not know how to classify it or whether they ought to approve it. *The Prince and the Pauper*, however, was perfectly safe and conventional.

No one at the time seemed to recognize that the novel is only a fairy tale. If they did, they seemed to want to believe it. The historical background is indeed accurate, and the message is clear; but the improbable premise of the story makes it insipid for any but the most unsophisticated reader or the most immature dreamer.

There is little of Mark Twain in it: a few jokes, one touching scene when the false prince recognizes his pauper mother, one delicious bit of boyish humor when the false prince admits having used the Great Seal of England to crack nuts with. And Mark Twain did include one reference to his own childhood in a peasant woman's giving the prince-as-pauper the task of drowning a litter of kittens, as Jane Clemens used to make Little Sam do. Otherwise the story is a children's masquerade.

The taste of the time is summed up in the New York *Herald*'s review of the book: "the characters of these two boys, twins in spirit, will rank with the purest and loveliest creations of child-life in the realm of fiction." The novel itself is about as unperceptive as that review. It does not solve the problem it puts—exchange of personality. Tom Canty and Edward VI are miserable in their new roles. The prince learns the superficialities of what it is to be poor and persecuted, but Tom Canty learns even less of what it is to be privileged. The boys may be pure and lovely, but they certainly are not such twins in spirit as Tom and Huck, or so universal.

The Prince and the Pauper had been published by James R. Osgood, of Boston. Elisha Bliss had died, and Mark Twain, who had never been entirely satisfied with Bliss's company—or, for that matter, with any other publishing firm, including his own—had listened to Howells' advice to patronize a Boston organization. Now Osgood was urging Mark to expand the Mississippi River articles into a book. Mark agreed to make another trip on the river to get material, and set out with Osgood and a stenographer in April, 1882.

They covered the Mississippi from New Orleans to St. Paul. Mark procured enough material for an additional forty-six chapters. He spent the rest of the year writing them. The book was published as *Life on the Mississippi* in May, 1883.

The new chapters unfortunately add little but information to the original, vibrant ones. Like piloting itself, the romance was gone. And the enthusiastic personal involvement of Mark Twain in the previously published Chapters 4–17 is missing from the later ones. Those *Atlantic* chapters still thrill, and make the book a masterpiece of autobiography as well as a magnificent picture of an American scene.

Like Antaeus, the giant of mythology whose strength was renewed whenever he touched his mother Earth, Mark Twain was reinspired every time he remembered or revisited the mighty river. He returned, eager to continue the sequel to *Tom Sawyer*, which was to be his greatest work.

9

FROM THE HEIGHTS TO THE DEPTHS

"Huck," says Tom at the end of *Tom Sawyer*, "we can't let you into the gang if you ain't respectable."

At the beginning of *The Adventures of Huckleberry Finn,* Huck says: "It was rough living in the house all the time, considering how dismal regular and decent the widow was in all her ways; and so when I couldn't stand it no longer, I lit out."

Huck had a chance that Mark Twain did not have, and that few persons have. He decided it as everyone dreams of doing. If for no other reason, then, *Huckleberry Finn* is a wish fulfillment, releasing the same tensions in the reader that the author has released for himself.

Mark Twain was nearing fifty. More than half the lifetime he could expect was spent. Where had it gone? What had been the real reward in terms of fulfilling himself, which is what saving his soul means to an agnostic like him? He might have said with Dante, "Midway in the course of this life I found myself in a dark wood."

True, he had found himself, but he had lost his way again. He felt forever committed to the prison of respectability. He was even afraid to break out of it. The Whittier Birthday speech had taught him that he must beware of freedom. Though he had been generously restored to favor in the *Atlantic* dinners, he could not forget that that gang had banished him because he was not respectable.

He was still an outcast and an exile searching for a world, a gang, in which he could be accepted on his own terms. More than that, he was struggling to find moral independence, true integrity. His return to the Mississippi River in 1882 had revived this tension. There long ago, in the pilothouse, he had felt free and in authority; in Hartford he was a moral slave.

The trip may also have suggested to him the symbol of a journey to express his wanderings in search of a spiritual home. A journey was the symbol Dante had used to externalize his conflict. So had Dante's guide Vergil in *The Aeneid*, and Vergil's master Homer in *The Odyssey*. Mark Twain had hinted at it in *Tom Sawyer*. Much as that creation fulfilled Mark's dream, it had not done the job thoroughly. There were more dark corners to be explored.

Tom Sawyer is a tentative soul. He is on the side of law and order. He abandons the bliss of the river island, for example, to return to his own funeral. His conscience wins. His one real journey into the cave is a symbol of the boy who felt himself an outcast wishing to return to the protection of the womb. Trapped there, and practically face to face with his deadly enemy Injun Joe, who symbolizes Tom's guilt at not being a "good boy," Tom nevertheless ingeniously escapes.

The same symbol appears in *The Odyssey* when Odysseus triumphs over his enemy Polyphemus and escapes by a stratagem from the cave. But Odysseus kills the Cyclops. There is no returning to the womb, or to the refuge of carefree boyhood. That is not home. Authority is not to be found in the past.

Tom Sawyer is rich and a hero at the end of the novel. But this conclusion satisfies only Tom. Huck, also a hero and rich, is dissatisfied. So with Mark Twain, who thought he would be content with social acceptance and wealth, but found that these acquisitions satisfied only the morals of society, not his own personal needs.

There had to be another resolution of the conflicts within Mark Twain. The fact that he began the history of Huckleberry Finn soon after completing *Tom Sawyer* shows that he had not expressed everything he needed to say about the human predicament. Although he laid the sequel aside, it could not have been completely absent from his thoughts; otherwise he would not have returned to it. Perhaps this long period of incubation is responsible for *The Adventures of Huckleberry Finn* becoming one of the great triumphs of the creative imagination. If nothing else of his survived, this work would be enough for Mark Twain to be ranked as a genius.

A genius is a creator. A work of genius is a transformation of the personal and specific into the general and abstract. The imagination of the genius is that part of him which works the transformation. Imagination comes partly from a keen emotional sensitivity to all experience, and partly from the mental ability to uncover the power of that experience to affect the senses—its essence.

The process can be compared to the refining of almost useless crude oil to obtain powerful gasoline. The crude oil is rid of particular characteristics until it has been transformed into a new and powerful substance. The French, incidentally, call gasoline *essence,* which literally means "being," true nature.

Once the genius has distilled the essence of his own experience, he has also provided the power for others to find meaning in their similar experiences. Hence the importance to the genius of creating a symbol to express the essence and be a bridge of communication between himself and others. The symbol represents the change of the ugly and familiar into the rich and new.

The essence of *Huckleberry Finn* is the conflict between the individual's own sense of justice and the arbitrary law of society. Whereas in *Tom Sawyer* the law wins, here integrity does. Huck decides he would rather go to hell than betray Jim, and incidentally himself, as the law says he should. And Huck's last words are: "I reckon I got to light out for the territory ahead of the rest, because Aunt Sally she's going to adopt me and sivilize me, and I can't stand it. I been there before."

The symbol of the orphan outcast is clearer in *Huckleberry Finn* than in *Tom Sawyer*. Huck's outcast father reappears in his life as an enemy who tries to trap him into servitude. This father, who represents authority, Huck sees as a horrible idol. Tom, on the other hand, knew no father and took as his authority the past he found in books and legends he did not understand. Tom did not escape tyranny, but Huck eluded it. When Huck learns that his father is dead, he is free of the enemy—completely free.

Then, too, there is the great recurring symbol of the journey. Huck's odyssey down the mighty river, which itself symbolizes life, is not a glamorous voyage as it was to Tom Sawyer. Rather, it is full of all the folly and dignity of man's struggle to assert himself.

The river is seen not as it was in *Life on the Mississippi*, as a hostile force to be reckoned with. Huck and Jim see it sympathetically. They are realists, not romantics like Pilot Samuel Clemens or Tom Sawyer, dreaming of the glories of the past. True, the river, like the sea of Odysseus, has its horrors, its Scylla and Charybdis, its Circe, its sirens, its Cyclops. But these are passed successfully or surmounted.

Neither does Huck crave the superiority the pilot and Tom Sawyer loved, because Huck is free of the need to avenge the tyranny of a god. Huck can adjust to his inferior, the runaway Jim. "It was fifteen minutes," he says, after having played a humiliating trick on Jim, "before I could work myself up to go and humble myself to a nigger; but I done it, and I warn't ever sorry for it afterward, neither. I didn't do him no more mean tricks." By sensing that there can be no true superiority of one human being over another, Huck gains authority by losing it. Now he can mature by being no longer at war with himself, for he had loved and respected Jim at the same time he had despised him as a slave. He has learned that the respectable and the disreputable are essentially the same. Thereafter, he can protect Jim instead of needing Jim's protection.

Tom Sawyer's reappearance in the concluding chapters of *Huckleberry Finn,* and his elaborate procedure for rescuing Jim, have been thought by some critics to be contrived and unsatisfactory. These critics apparently do not appreciate the great fun of the episode or see its symbolism.

Jim, who is free of a moral sense, has been betrayed by the mountebanks who have joined him and Huck on the river. Thought to be a runaway slave, Jim is loosely chained and casually guarded until his supposed owner comes to claim him. As the realist Huck points out, releasing him is a simple matter. Tom, however, romanticizes Jim into a composite of all state prisoners of history, and invents a ludicrously intricate way of liberating him.

Tom knows all along that Jim has been freed from literal slavery, just as Jim is free from the spiritual slavery of the moral sense. But Tom, who represents the social order, wishes Jim imprisoned by the moral sense, just as Tom himself has been.

The unnecessary rescue symbolizes man's difficulty in getting free of the false, imaginary chains of the moral sense—that mighty fortress in which Mark Twain saw himself arbitrarily confined. Mark felt that he, like Jim, had been betrayed into that captivity by impostors, and that a childish society had invented needless chains and spiders and snakes to torture him there. All he needed to liberate himself was recognition of the truth that he was a free soul.

At the end of the journey, Huck finds a home in the literal sense. He does not need it because he has found himself—a home in the broader sense. His is the dauntless spirit of man. He cannot rest. Like Odysseus, he puts his oar on his shoulder and begins his journey once more —to "the territory," toward the West, the eternal symbol of freedom and opportunity.

It is an ending that Mark Twain dreamed might be his, for he, too, had headed westward from the river in a vain search for treasures upon earth. But Mark Twain was never to stop wandering. "A man," he would write, "is never anything but what his outside influences have made him." He himself never found what he projected for Huckleberry Finn. If he had, he would have ceased creating.

Chapters of *Huckleberry Finn* (the Shepherdson-Grangerford feud and King Sollermun) appeared in the December, 1884, and January, 1885, issues of the *Century* magazine before the book itself was published. These chapters whetted the appetite of the public, as did Mark Twain's public readings from the manuscript. The advance sale was over forty thousand copies.

Immediately after the book's publication in February, 1885, the library of Concord, Massachusetts, banned it from its shelves. Concord was the cradle of American liberty, but it was also the home of Louisa May Alcott—who condemned the book's vulgarity—and of other heirs of the high thinkers who had made the town famous again a generation before. Mark Twain greeted the news with joy. "A rattling tiptop puff," he called it, "that will sell twenty-five thousand copies for us sure." Other libraries followed Concord's example. Meanwhile, the Concord Free Trade Club made Mark Twain an honorary member.

The librarians objected to Huck's moral code, which is actually a plea for tolerance and against oppression, and which is psychologically accurate in the circumstances. The critics neglected the book; some even thought Mark Twain was finished as a writer. The story was too unrefined for that genteel age to recognize it as a masterpiece and one of the world's great novels.

Like *Tom Sawyer,* it was a startling departure from conventional fiction. It was, for instance, the first novel to be written in the American common speech. It contained no love affair and no heroine. It dealt with raw, rough life, and made sordid and uncouth characters commanding and even pitiful. It did no moralizing; Huck reports objectively and unemotionally such an incident as the shooting of old Boggs, then adds: "I went to the circus." And it made the "wicked" Huck lovable. The hypocrisy of the genteel age was never more spotlighted than by its official rejection of this encyclopedia of humanity and of human kindness.

Huckleberry Finn was published by the firm of Charles L. Webster and Company, of New York. Mark Twain had severed connections with Osgood, though he continued to be fond of him as a person. Webster, the husband of Mark's niece (Pamela's daughter), had been engaged by Mark to manage an enterprise for chalk reproduction of engravings. This had been brought to Mark's attention by

Dan Slote, and Mark had invested heavily in it. It was soon superseded by brass-plate engraving. Mark lost his money, and Webster his job.

Mark then got Osgood to make Webster his subscription manager for the sale of *Life on the Mississippi.* Webster thus became the actual publisher of that book. Later, Mark made him his own business manager. By the time *Huckleberry Finn* was finished, Webster had an office and staff of his own, and was being backed by Mark Twain's inspiration and capital. Mark directed him in canvassing the advance sale of *Huckleberry Finn,* and Webster, an able young man, got the book selling at the rate of ten thousand copies a month, after publication. Mark congratulated him and decided that thereafter he would be his own publisher.

A publisher, of course, has to have profitable manuscripts to issue as books. Luck played into Mark's hands by putting in his way a book that for the time being was to outsell *Huckleberry Finn.* He overheard that ex-President General Ulysses S. Grant was preparing to publish his memoirs. He lost no time in getting to the General.

While he was a correspondent in Washington in 1868 he had met Grant. The General had allowed Mark to interview him, but Mark had been so overpowered by the grim figure that he could think of nothing to ask him.

"General," he said at last, "I seem to be embarrassed. Are you?"

After that, Grant actually smiled, and the interview went well.

Mark met Grant a second time at a welcome that Chicago was giving the General. When they shook hands, Grant said: "Mr. Clemens, I am not embarrassed. Are you?"

That evening, at a banquet for Grant, Mark gave one

of his most famous speeches. He pictured Grant in his cradle, so unaware of his coming greatness that his only concern was to get his big toe into his mouth. Then, after a splendidly timed pause, Mark added: "And if the child is but the father of the man, there are mighty few who will doubt that he succeeded!"

Grant laughed until he cried. He went up to congratulate Mark Twain. "You tore me all to pieces," he said.

From that time on, they were good friends.

Now Mark approached the bankrupt and ailing former President and reminded him that even though he had promised his memoirs to the Century Company, he had earlier promised them to Mark. Furthermore, Mark offered Grant better terms and a larger guarantee of sales than Century had.

Grant hesitated, thinking Mark's offer too generous. Then he realized that he had not much longer to live or to pay off his colossal debts. He signed Mark's contract on February 27, 1885. Then, against the pain of the cancer that was destroying him, he labored to complete his manuscript. Mark Twain gave him moral encouragement. Three days before he died, Grant finished the book.

Webster and Company moved to larger offices to prepare for canvassing the sale and the publication of the *Memoirs*. Grant's death greatly increased the orders. One year after the contract had been signed, Mark Twain's firm paid Mrs. Grant $200,000 in royalties, the largest sum ever paid an author up to that time. The company later paid her about $250,000 more.

The year had been a grand one for Mark, even though his preoccupation with the Grant book had kept him from writing. In November he celebrated his fiftieth birthday. He was at the height of his fame and his prosperity.

Again he was enjoying his home and his family. The big house had been designed to suit his tastes and had such bizarre features as a window over a fireplace, so that Mark could watch the flames rise and the snow fall at the same time. It had a porch built to resemble a steamboat deck, and a balcony like a pilothouse. In its secluded billiard room Mark could swear while at his favorite game, if he felt like it. In his own room was the enormous Venetian bed, carved with cherubs and garlands, which he had bought in Italy. He loved to work lying in this bed with his head at the foot so that he could see the mahogany decorations on the headboard.

Another daughter, Jane, called Jean, had arrived in 1880 and now was old enough to share with her two sisters in the family fun. Mark organized a Saturday Morning Club for his girls and those of the Nook Farm neighbors, and procured guest lecturers for it, including himself and Bret Harte. The girls frequently got up amateur theatricals in which Mark sometimes acted a part. Mark read aloud to his family some of his works in progress, particularly *The Prince and the Pauper* and *Huckleberry Finn*, and listened to his daughters' opinions. One of the whimsical bedtime stories he told them was published long after his death in *Letters from the Earth* as "A Cat-Tale." Mark had loved kittens since his babyhood, and there were always plenty around the house.

Quite a part of the household were the faithful family servants: Katy Leary, who was with the Clemenses for over thirty years and whose memoir of Mark Twain is an important reference for his biography; Patrick McAleer, their coachman for twenty-five years; and George, Mark's Negro valet. Mark took an interest in even temporary help, and once, through a trick, got one of the three maids a fine husband.

Mark was probably the first author to own and use a fountain pen, as he had been to use a typewriter. He could not keep his hands off new inventions any more than he could out of business ventures. When the two went together, there was no restraining him. The fact never dawned on him that he had no skill whatever in making money out of anything but himself.

When Orion turned up in Hartford with a new kind of paddle wheel, Mark backed him. That failed. He put all his cash into a crackpot steam generator, and lost it. Then he sank $30,000 in a steam pulley, and after that, $25,000 in a new scheme for marine telegraphy. And so on. But when Alexander Graham Bell pleaded with him to buy stock in the telephone at $25 a share, Mark absolutely refused. The first telephone installed in a private house, however, was in Mark Twain's.

By 1885 he was involved in financing a typesetting machine that had been invented by James W. Paige and was being developed at the Colt arms factory in Hartford. Having been for years an expert typesetter, Mark thought he knew all about the process. He failed to see, however, that Paige was a perfectionist and that the machine was too delicate to stand up under the hard use it would be subject to.

Just as in his mining ventures, Mark was counting his profits but ignoring the cost of getting them. By 1887, he said, he would have a thousand of the Paige machines rented out all over the world at a profit of $2,500,000. But the machine kept breaking down, or Paige would think of some new device to increase its efficiency. It was draining an average of $3,000 a month from Mark's bank account. By 1887 it had cost him $80,000. In the meantime, the sturdier and more practical Mergenthaler linotype machine had been put on the market.

Still, Paige kept promising to get his machine working, and Mark kept believing that it would be superior to any other. Frantically he tried to raise capital in order to protect his own investment, but the financiers he approached would not believe in the $55,000,000 a year earnings Mark projected. They said obliquely that they had no doubt as to the future of the Paige machine, but for the present they preferred to put their money into the Mergenthaler. Early in 1891, Mark finally threw in the towel after the $190,000 he had already wasted.

In order to get enough money to continue financing Paige, Mark Twain had had to produce another book. His other business interests had kept him too occupied to produce more than a few short stories and speeches. Of these, only "The History of a Campaign That Failed," about his brief Civil War soldiering, is significant. None of them brought him anything like the income he needed for even his living expenses.

In 1886 he had begun "a book whose scene is laid far back in the twilight of tradition," as he described the project in a letter to Webster. He was too busy with other interests to work at it steadily. When Howells visited Hartford, as he did frequently then, Mark would read him what chapters had been finished. Howells praised them and encouraged Mark to continue. Even so, he procrastinated until the summer of 1888, when he was so alarmed at the state of his finances that he worked feverishly to complete the book in order to get some income from it. By the fall of that year even his children knew money was scarce in the household. Not until the spring of 1889, however, was the book done. It was published by Webster and Company in December of that year under the title of *A Connecticut Yankee in King Arthur's Court.*

During the fall of 1884 and into the winter of 1885, Mark Twain had teamed with George Washington Cable, a popular writer of stories about the Old South, for a tour of readings from their works. This form of entertainment was almost as popular as lectures. Mark earned some much-needed money from the tour, even though he thought it beneath him, in spite of pleasing his audiences.

Early in 1885, Mark had been inspecting a copy of Sir Thomas Malory's *Morte d'Arthur* in a bookstore. Cable bought it for him and highly recommended it to him. Mark loved this fifteenth-century compilation of all the tales and legends of local heroes that for nearly a thousand years had been growing up around the central figure of King Arthur. Malory's lyrical style and his gift for simple, direct narration delighted Mark. Almost at once he began jotting into his notebook ideas for a story about a nineteenth-century factory foreman transplanted in a dream into sixth-century England.

In his *Autobiography,* Mark Twain wrote that the book "was an attempt to imagine, and after a fashion set forth, the hard conditions of life for the laboring and defenseless poor in bygone times in England, and incidentally contrast these conditions with those under which the civil and ecclesiastical pets of privilege lived in those times." Hank Morgan, the Yankee, is the spokesman for Mark Twain's vehement sentiments in favor of American democracy of the Andrew Jackson variety. These sentiments had made him partisan in the 1884 election campaign, during which he had expressed his vigorously independent political feelings. He had changed a great deal since he expressed his contempt for universal suffrage in *The Gilded Age*.

Mark Twain was now on the side of progressive socialism as a system of society. He had been outraged by the repressive measures of the Russian, and even the German, autocracy, and by the predatory rule of the Belgians in the Congo. He was also influenced by the reform economics and the faith in human nature of Henry George's *Progress and Poverty*. He confessed to being fascinated by Edward Bellamy's *Looking Backward,* a utopia written, like the *Yankee,* in dream form. From almost complete indifference to matters of government and economics, Mark had shifted to a liberal stand in these fields.

The novel is a satire both on the conditions of King Arthur's time (actually Mark Twain was writing about the Middle Ages) and on the romantic nostalgia that had glamorized them. During the latter half of the nineteenth century everything connected with the King Arthur story had been sentimentalized and moralized and idealized to a nauseating degree. Tennyson's *Idylls of the King* had pictured the Knights of the Round Table as a club of pious prep-school boys. William Morris and the Pre-Raphaelite painters had made no home seem respectable without at least one reproduction of a languorous medieval maiden or of a Christlike Sir Galahad. Hearing Richard Wagner's *Parsifal* was considered as obligatory as daily prayers, and not everyone perceived the sensuousness of his interpretation of the Tristan and Isolde story. As in *The Prince and the Pauper,* Mark Twain was debunking the past as a model and exposing the foolishness of turning to it for authority. The human race, he insinuated, was just as damned then as before or since. As he was to write later in *Joan of Arc,* another of his excursions into the past: "There is no way of accounting for people. You have to take them as they are."

This essence of humor makes the *Yankee* a hilarious book. The ideas and theories Mark Twain labors in it are now old hat, for most of them have become standard practices, but the farcical anachronisms are still amusing: Sir Launcelot jousting on a high-wheeled bicycle, for example, or knights in armor advertising "Persimmon's Soap" (a satire on the ubiquitous advertisements of Pears' Soap) by means of sandwich signs.

Hank Morgan, "Sir Boss," is a grown-up Huck Finn, whose comments on medieval chivalry are as fresh as Huck's on life in the 1840's. "Well," says Hank, "it was touching to see the queen blush and smile, and look embarrassed, and happy, and fling furtive glances at Sir Launcelot that would have got him shot in Arkansas, to a dead certainty." Hank compares the involved and endless tales of knight errantry he has to hear to literary German: "I was standing in the awful presence of the mother of the German Language. . . . Whenever the literary German dives into a sentence, that is the last you are going to see of him till he emerges on the other side of the Atlantic with his verb in his mouth."

The *Yankee* is hardly a good novel, if indeed it was ever intended to be, but it is very good fun. The English, nevertheless, were incensed at Mark Twain's ridicule of their sacred figures of legend, and he had to make many alterations in the text for a British edition. The fun still goes on; the *Yankee* has been dramatized, turned into one of the best of all musical comedies, made into a motion picture twice (once with Will Rogers giving a magnificent interpretation of Hank Morgan), and now appears from time to time on television. Although vastly inferior as a work of art to *Tom Sawyer* and *Huckleberry Finn*, it ranks with them as Mark Twain's most popular and enduring work.

The original edition of the *Yankee* was illustrated by Dan Carter Beard, who later founded the American Boy Scouts. Although his drawings are in the style of the 1880's, they are still part of the fun. Beard used a real Connecticut Yankee as a model, and famous people—Queen Victoria, Kaiser Wilhelm, Sarah Bernhardt, the Prince of Wales (later King Edward VII), and Jay Gould—as models for the knights and ladies of King Arthur's court.

The success of the *Yankee* was but a thumb in the disintegrating dike of Mark Twain's fortunes. The publishing company was not making money or increasing its prestige; in fact, new books contracted for had to be financed on borrowed funds. Charles Webster collapsed from overwork, had to retire from the firm, and died in April, 1891. His successor, Fred J. Hall, was too young and inexperienced to do more than keep the enterprise barely afloat. Impatient as always, and now desperate, Mark Twain himself did not help matters much.

Mark Twain was again wholly dependent on his pen for a living, but he was too tired to invent a good book, and he was suffering from excruciating rheumatism. He threw together some old stories and sketches, added a prose version of the wretched play he and Howells had made out of the further adventures of Colonel Sellers, and published them under the title of that piece, *The American Claimant*. It is the worst of all the things he allowed to see print.

When *McClure's* magazine offered him a thousand dollars apiece for six travel articles, Mark Twain decided to take his whole family for an indefinite stay in Europe, where living was much cheaper.

Sadly they closed the Hartford house, and sailed on the *Gascogne* on June 6, 1891.

10

THE BOTTOMLESS PIT

It was a shaky party that arrived in France. Mark's arm was practically useless from rheumatism. Livy had developed symptoms of heart disease. Susy was not yet over the nervous breakdown caused by homesickness during her freshman year at Bryn Mawr. They spent the next year very quietly.

By the summer of 1892 they were all in better health. Mark made a flying trip back to America to try once more to save the Paige investment; then they settled at Bad Nauheim, Germany. Mark's arm permitted him to write again. He turned out several articles and stories, and began work on *Tom Sawyer Abroad* and *Those Extraordinary Twins* (the original form of *Pudd'nhead Wilson*).

The Prince of Wales, who was recuperating at Bad Nauheim from a winter of dissipation, asked the British ambassador to arrange an introduction for Mark. When they met, the Prince took Mark's arm, and they strolled up and down, talking cordially. As they were parting, Mark expressed his appreciation of the royal courtesy.

"It is a pleasure," the Prince said, "to have met you—again."

Mark did not understand the "again."

"Don't you remember," said the Prince, "the day in London when you were on the top of a bus and I was heading a procession and you had on your new overcoat with flap pockets?"

It was a great compliment from a prince to a pauper, for it showed that the future King Edward VII remembered a humorous article Mark Twain had written five years before, in which he claimed to have met the Prince as described.

Later the Prince asked him to supper, following the example of the German Kaiser, who had entertained Mark at dinner the previous winter.

In the autumn the family moved on to Settignano, a quiet, lovely village on a hilltop overlooking Florence. Livy's health improved there, and Mark found the place ideal for writing. He finished *Tom Sawyer Abroad,* a silly, contrived story of a balloon trip to the Sahara with Tom, Huck, and Jim; and began converting the mistake of *Those Extraordinary Twins* into another form. He also wrote an excellent short story, "The £1,000,000 Bank Note," and began the *Personal Recollections of Joan of Arc.*

Another ray of hope for the Paige typesetter brought Mark to America in March, 1893. He returned to Italy in May, optimistic about the prospects. Then news came from Fred Hall that Charles L. Webster and Company was almost bankrupt, owing to the financial depression which had made it virtually impossible to borrow money. Mark walked the floor at night, worrying about where his next dollar would come from. The depression had made the typesetter stock unsalable. In desperation he returned to New York in late August to try to save his own royalties from the wreckage of the publishing firm. He could afford only a $1.50-a-day room on the fourth floor at his favorite club, The Players.

In January, 1888, Augustin Daly, one of the principal theatrical producers in New York, had invited Mark Twain to a luncheon at Delmonico's along with Edwin Booth, Thomas Bailey Aldrich, General William Tecumseh Sherman, Professor Brander Matthews of Columbia University, and eleven other men of reputation in the theater or in literature. The purpose was to discuss plans for a club of limited membership, where gentlemen of the arts could gather and which would lend dignity to distinguished professions not yet recognized by snobbish society leaders. Edwin Booth had bought a large house at 16 Gramercy Park, had it remodeled by America's then foremost architect, Stanford White, completely furnished it, and installed in it his own outstanding collections of books, pictures, and memorabilia of the theater.

On New Year's Eve that year, Booth presented the house to the club, for which Aldrich had suggested the name, The Players. The guests at Daly's luncheon were the founding members. At once it became, and has since remained, one of the most famous and delightful clubs in the world, where the company, the conversation, and the entertainment probably surpass even the celebrated eighteenth-century "The Club" of Dr. Johnson, Boswell, Goldsmith, Garrick, Burke, Reynolds, and other leading lights of that era.

Mark Twain was frequently there, to lunch or dine at the Round Table, play billiards, or join the exclusively masculine company around the gorgeous main fireplace in the evening, and entertain them with ribald stories. His cue, and his portrait by Gordon Stevenson still decorate the billiard room, and his witticisms are still quoted there.

The society at The Players greatly relieved Mark

Twain's distress of mind during the agonizing days of the summer of 1893, when he saw crashing around him the world he had dreamed so long to make. Then, at almost the blackest hour of his despair, a friend of Mark's casually introduced him to a man who would restore his finances and his spirits.

This man was Henry H. Rogers, a director of the Standard Oil Company, then at the height of its fearful power as a ruthless monopoly. Rogers, who highly admired Mark Twain's works, offered his skill as a financial pirate to extricate the desperate author from his predicament. Mark overlooked his disapproval of the methods of the Standard Oil Company, and gave Rogers authority to handle everything. Rogers staved off ruin for another six months.

Meanwhile, to forget his troubles, Mark plunged into the social whirl of the city to such an extent that his fellow Players dubbed him "the Belle of New York."

In spite of all Rogers could and did do, Charles L. Webster and Company failed on April 18,1894, for $100,000. Its principal creditor, the Mount Morris Bank, had demanded that the banks' loans be paid at once. Rogers negotiated a settlement of fifty cents on the dollar with the creditors, but Mark Twain determined that they should be paid in full.

Mark felt relieved that at last something had been settled, and he was touched by the immediate assistance he got from his friends, who sent him checks amounting to over two thousand dollars. The New York *Herald* launched a public relief fund for him, proclaiming it was every American's patriotic duty to contribute to the relief of "the greatest humorist of the age." Mark would have none of it. The failure was a personal matter to him, especially as it involved Livy's own money. She could not, as she wrote her sister, "get away from the feeling that business failure means disgrace." Mark trusted that if he had built a fortune once, he could do so again, even though he was now old and in poor health.

There was a chance that the Paige typesetter would stand the test the Chicago *Times-Herald* was giving it, and would bail Mark out. *Tom Sawyer Abroad* had been published by Webster and Company on the day it failed, and would bring some income. Mark arranged for the publication of *Pudd'nhead Wilson* with his former publishers in Hartford, and returned to Europe to write as hard as he could. Then in December the Paige machine collapsed for the last time. All Mark could give Livy as a present on their twenty-fifth wedding anniversary the following February was a silver five-franc piece.

Pudd'nhead Wilson, which had been published in November, 1894, shows the effects of its having been written while the author was under a strain. It is the most poorly executed of Mark Twain's major works, and the least rounded out. In places it seems like a mere outline for a novel, lacking the development of characters, scenes, motivations, and reactions that would make the story more believable.

Mark Twain was always a conscious artist, planning and polishing his work carefully, and then studiously revising it himself and with consideration of the opinions of Livy, Howells, Edmund Clarence Stedman, and others. But *Pudd'nhead Wilson* reads as if it had been dashed off at top speed, and some of its meanings are therefore ambiguous. The reader is not sure, for example, whether the extraordinary Italian twins are two separate bodies or the two-headed monster with which Mark Twain started the book but which he removed into a separate story.

Even with these flaws, *Puddn'head Wilson* has an interesting, involved plot, and creates its own atmosphere—the isolated, dusty Missouri village of Dawson's Landing on the Mississippi River in the years from 1830 to 1850. Mark Twain evokes the village's intolerance, its superstitions, and its petty intrigues as brilliantly as he did the locales of *Tom Sawyer* and *Huckleberry Finn.* This was a setting, and its inhabitants were characters, the like of which he had seen and known and begrudgingly loved.

It is a sincere work of protest against oppression, against the hideous injustice of slavery and race prejudice, against narrow provincialism. For the first time, Mark Twain was expressing publicly some of his ideas about the nature of man and his place in the universe. These he had uttered privately in a paper he had read to the Hartford Monday Evening Club in the winter of 1883. He was to develop them into his credo, which he allowed to be printed privately in 1906 as *What Is Man?* for circulation among his friends.

The essence of his deterministic philosophy is that all influences on a person's conduct come from outside him. Mark expounded that man acts only to content himself, but he tempered this belief with a kind of categorical imperative: "Diligently train your ideals upward and still upward toward a summit where you will find your chiefest pleasure in conduct which, while contenting you, will be sure to confer benefits upon your neighbor and the community." A man's temperament, he continued, is what he is. He can obey no command contrary to that temperament. Man is born what he is; what he accomplishes is due to training.

In *Pudd'nhead Wilson,* the symbol Mark Twain chose to express these convictions is the fingerprints of two babies—one born a slave, the other born heir to the fortune and traditions of an outstanding family. The infants are switched by the ambitious mother of the slave child, and are trained accordingly. Then their true identities are revealed by Wilson, who has kept the fingerprints. The one trained as a slave is a slave in every sense, however legally free he once was and has since become. The real slave, trained as a spoiled, selfish gentleman, becomes a valuable slave, and is sold down the river.

Many of Mark Twain's philosophical ideas now appeared as David ("Pudd'nhead") Wilson's aphorisms at the beginning of every chapter in the novel. Possibly the most famous is: "Training is everything. The peach was once a bitter almond; cauliflower is nothing but cabbage with a college education." The most bitter, reflecting his opinion of "the damned human race" is: "If you pick up a starving dog and make him prosperous, he will not bite you. This is the principal difference between a dog and a man." He expressed his own creed in another: "Let us endeavor so to live that when we come to die even the undertaker will be sorry."

Wilson expresses the Mark Twain of the period of financial ruin as clearly as Tom or Huck represent him at the top of success. Mark's financial failure damaged the secret image he had of himself. Wilson lives in disgrace at Dawson's Landing because of a witty remark of his that none of the stupid yokels could understand—a symbol of Mark Twain's unrewarding investments. After many years Wilson redeems himself through his intelligence in a crisis. Meanwhile he composes the aphorisms that utter Mark Twain's own beliefs and indicate the growing disillusionment of both men. Genius of Mark Twain's type cannot help identifying with the characters it creates. Out of the materials of his own life he forged his art.

His business failure also injured his work. The *Personal Recollections of Joan of Arc,* which he composed during his economic exile in Europe and finished early in 1895, is sadly uninspired. He had been captivated by the story of Joan since the day over forty years before, when the page from a book about her blew across his path in Hannibal. Much as he loved her character and much as he studied her career, he let her elude him. Possibly he put himself too much in her position, conceiving himself as a martyr also. But a maiden's form was no embodiment for the spirit of Mark Twain.

The long book merely fleshes out the known facts of Joan's fifteenth-century life by developing personages who, in history, are little more than names, and by painting backdrops for the action. It adds some characters, but they are puppets in fancy medieval dress. Either history or Mark Twain works their strings. The exception is the Paladin, who wears armor but is straight out of the nineteenth-century American West.

Thoroughly as Mark Twain investigated the background of the story, he speculated not at all on the mystery of Joan and her career. This omission is strange in view of his skepticism about miracles and divine inspiration. Perhaps he accepted Joan's "voices" as a form of mental telepathy, in which he firmly believed. More likely, regarding her as an example of the unblemished womanhood that was his ideal, he thought she needed no explication. In any event, he added nothing to a modern understanding of either the maid or her story. Of all the brilliant authors who have dealt with the subject, Mark Twain succeeded the least well at interpreting it.

Once *Joan of Arc* was finished, Mark Twain sailed for America to negotiate its publishing contract with Harper's, in whose magazine it had been serialized. Henry Rogers had worked out a plan whereby Harper Brothers could purchase the Webster and Company book contracts; he needed Mark to help him secure the American Company ones for Harper's. Harper's was to be the publisher of all Mark Twain's works from then on until their copyrights expired; thereafter it was to be the licensor of the name Mark Twain, which Mark later registered as a trademark, to other publishers. Since Harper Brothers was one of the foremost and most reliable of all publishing firms, this arrangement of Rogers' guaranteed Mark Twain an income averaging $50,000 a year.

During this trip, Mark conceived the idea of a tour of lectures around the world. He hated lecturing, but he saw the tour as the only quick way to pay off his debts. He could not endure being poor and having to economize and curtail his generosity to others. "The offspring of riches," he wrote, "is pride, vanity, ostentation, arrogance, tyranny." But he also wrote: "The offspring of poverty: greed, sordidness, envy, hate, malice, cruelty, meanness, lying, shirking, cheating, stealing, murder."

He arranged with Major J. B. Pond, who had managed his tour of readings with Cable, to arrange this tour of the world. Then he returned to Europe to bring his family back to Quarry Farm. On July 14, 1895, he left Elmira with Livy and Clara.

The tour took them through the northern states to Vancouver; then to Australia, New Zealand, Ceylon, India, South Africa. It was a hard trip in spite of the welcome and the success Mark encountered everywhere, and much of the time he was troubled with painful boils. The trio arrived in England on July 31, 1896, where they expected to be met by Susy and Jean and Katy Leary.

Instead, they were greeted with news that Susy was sick. Two weeks later came a cable that she had died of meningitis.

Susy had been Mark's favorite daughter. She was the most like him, being intelligent, independent, witty, and something of a writer. She also had a fine soprano voice that might have been suitable for opera if she could have developed the physique to project it and sustain a heavy role. Like all Mark's children, however, she was sickly and of a fragile nervous constitution.

If Mark had ever blamed himself for other deaths in the family, his self-reproach was nothing to what it was now. His biographer Paine states that Mark "charged himself categorically as being wholly and solely responsible for the tragedy, detailing step by step with fearful reality his mistakes and weaknesses which had led to their downfall, the separation from Susy, and this final incredible disaster."

For Susy's headstone at Elmira, Mark Twain adapted the lines of the Australian poet Robert Richardson:

Warm summer sun shine kindly here;
Warm southern wind blow softly here;
Green sod above, lie light, lie light—
Good night, dear heart, good night, good night.

He never got over his grief. Nor was it the last time he was to suffer. The remaining fourteen years of his life saw him heroically trying to rise above them externally, but internally sinking deeper and deeper into pessimism and despair.

11

THE PHOENIX

Livy and Clara had rushed home in the vain hope of seeing Susy alive. After her burial they returned to England with Jean and Katy Leary. The family took a house in a remote part of London and gave the address to only a few close friends. Mourning their loss, they lived in almost total seclusion until the following summer. Mark brooded over his bad luck to the point that he believed he was infecting others with it. He was close to insanity.

To forget Susy's death he worked at many projects. He also wanted to vindicate himself as a writer and to repair the shattered image of himself. What occupied him on the surface was a travel book about his around-the-world lecture tour, but he was doing this only for money. When it was published in November, 1897, as *Following the Equator,* it proved to be the dullest of his books.

The other projects lay under the surface. These were begun to sublimate his intense grief in an artistic form. He was struggling to find some explanation for what had happened to him. "Why am I robbed," he wrote to Howells, "and who is benefited?"

What haunted him was the belief that his calamities had been his fault. Deep within him remained the Calvinism which had been so uncompromisingly imposed on him when he was a child. He had rebelled against it, and thought he had discarded it. In his prosperity he had said to Joseph Twichell during their tour in 1878: "Joe, I don't believe in your religion at all. I've been living a lie whenever I pretended to." Now guilt, the essence of Calvinism, again plagued him. As he watched Queen Victoria's Diamond Jubilee procession on June 23, 1897, he could not help thinking of the dreadful Last Judgment. Could God be kind to him then after having been so cruel before?

He began to expand the deterministic philosophy he had propounded in his Monday Evening Club address into a system that might prove there is no such thing as free will, and that man is helpless in a fixed, cause-and-effect universe. He was entering a plea of Not Guilty, not to blame for anything he had done, not responsible for his catastrophes. The whole awful experience must somehow have been a dream.

These are the premises of the several desperate attempts he made to express his feelings. But he could not then draw logical conclusions from them. The experience was too immediate. He was too close to it to be able to find its meaning. His inability to find a symbol for his emotions increased his despair. He was afraid he was losing, or had lost, his talent. Yet he was under a violent compulsion to write, write, write. The meaning had to be found.

The enormous number of words he poured into manuscripts he could not finish shows his agony of mind. All of them are stories designed in the framework of a dream, to prove that a dream is the only reality.

While he was struggling, his mind returned to the "Carnival of Crime" story of nearly twenty years before, and the question of man's dual nature. In his *Notebook* he wrote: "We have a spiritualized self which can detach itself. It has a memory of its own and can recall its acts. What I took to be unreality and called Dreams for want of a truthfuller name . . . is merely my ordinary body and mind freed from clogging flesh and become a spiritualized body and mind." He put great emphasis on the "truthfulness" of dreams, calling them "that other person who is in me."

All these fragments contain representations of Mark Twain's own disasters, particularly his financial ruin and the loss of Susy. One protagonist dreams that he has burned up his house and his family; another, that he has been ruined by a relative. Never is the fault his own. In the most fully developed one occurs the symbol of a family's fearful voyage on a ship lost in the Antarctic, with no destination and pursued by a ghastly monster of the deep that is trying to destroy it.

The story breaks off with the captain of the ship quelling a mutiny with the words: "If it is God's will that we pull through, we pull through—otherwise not. . . . We are going ahead, and do our best to fetch up somewhere." Mark Twain was determined to find a way out of his despair. There also emerges a faint outline of the symbol that eventually would solve his problem of communication. This is a mysterious being called the "Superintendent of Dreams," who plays mischievous tricks on the passengers and the crew.

In his further gropings toward a symbol, Mark Twain made a pitiful effort to return to his former greatness by reviving Tom Sawyer and Huck Finn and Hannibal, Missouri—the personifications of his golden boyhood and his dream of home. He got nowhere. But he introduces into this environment a mysterious stranger who performs all sorts of tricks to get admiration, show his strength, free others from pain, and do all the other things Mark Twain himself liked to do. This stranger is young Satan.

In Mark Twain's time many persons believed in the existence of Satan as a spiritual being. Their theory was that if God exists, then His opposite must also exist. They accepted the biblical myth in which Satan was originally the brightest of all the angels. Because of Satan's pride and his envy of God's supremacy, he rebelled. He was cast out of heaven, but was given permission by God to exercise a sort of government in the world, where he roves seeking to destroy men by involving them in guilt. His function is to tempt men to wickedness and thus test their devotion to God. The legend leads to speculation as to whether Evil is supreme in the world, with Good struggling to overcome it, or whether the reverse is true.

Like many another genius, Mark Twain believed himself to be a sort of mysterious stranger on the earth. In the fragment dealing with Satan's visit to Hannibal, the stranger asks the earthlings: "How do you know when a comet has swum into your system? Merely by your eye or your telescope—but I, I hear a brilliant far stream of sound come winding through the firmament of majestic sounds and I know the splendid stranger is there without looking." Samuel Clemens had been born with a comet in the sky, and Mark Twain was to die with it again in the heavens.

He felt close to Satan, a genius like himself, but immune to guilt and spared the burden of a moral sense. He pitied Satan. "I have no prejudice against him," he wrote in 1899. "It may even be that I lean a little his way, on account of his not having a fair show. All religions issue bibles against him, but we never hear *his* side. . . . I would like to see him." Gradually Mark was coming to identify himself with Satan, the mysterious stranger.

The symbol now was clear. The final answer came with

Mark Twain's transforming the Hannibal of his youth into the sixteenth-century German town of Eseldorf (Jackassville). So remote now seemed the idyllic years of his carefree youth; so damned and stupid now appeared the human race. The Tom and Huck and Joe Harper of *Tom Sawyer* become three medieval German boys, but they are passive now, not active. Nothing is their fault. "Eseldorf," Mark says of the new Hannibal, "was a paradise for us boys." Into this paradise came Satan—called Philip Traum (Dream)—to work all kinds of tricks and to demonstrate that, try as he will, man cannot control his fate.

This powerful story, a triumph of the transforming imagination, evolved out of Mark Twain's agonizing attempts to externalize his suffering. He began the quest for this release of tension soon after Susy's death. Just when he completed it is not clear. The manuscript was found among his papers after his death, and was published as *The Mysterious Stranger* in 1916. It contains Mark Twain's final conclusions about the human condition.

"Every man," Satan explains to the boys, "is a suffering-machine and a happiness-machine combined." The machines supposedly balance each other, but "sometimes a man's make and disposition are such that his misery-machine is able to do nearly all the business." Such a person has only a vague idea of what happiness is and he brings misfortune on himself. Life to him is a disaster.

Men are foolish. The only sense they have is the moral sense. Man is to Satan as a red spider, a creature Mark Twain loathed, is to an elephant—ignored. The elephant cannot bother to do the spider any mischief, but might do it a service if it cost nothing. So, Satan says, "I have done men good service, but no ill turns."

Man's trivial mind patches things together for a result,

but Satan's mind creates. God does not foreordain man's career; it is ordered by man's own acts, each one of which is determined by the one preceding it. Satan alone can free man from the consequences of man's "first childish act."

Satan, the realist, demonstrates the futility of civilization. Out of all those civilizations which have flourished and fallen, only the present and supposedly the best one, he says, "ever invented any sweeping and adequate way to kill people." All civilization has done is to perpetuate a master-versus-slave system in one form or another. The human race lives "a life of continuous and uninterrupted self-deception."

When Satan takes his leave of Eseldorf, he gives his solution to the problem: "Life itself is only a vision, a dream. . . . Nothing exists; all is a dream. . . . Nothing exists save empty space—and you!"

"He vanished," says the boy narrator, "and left me appalled; for I knew, and realized, that all he had said was true."

Gradually the gloom lifted. By the spring of 1897 Mark Twain could manage a smile. Following up a rumor that Mark was ill, a young reporter called for an interview. He showed his cabled instructions: "If Twain very ill, send five hundred words; if dead, one thousand."

Mark told him: "You don't need as much as that. Just say the report of my death has been grossly exaggerated."

The family moved to Switzerland for the summer, then to Vienna. There, in a palatial hotel suite, Mark Twain held court through the following year. The Queen of Romania was among his friends, along with the leading authors, painters, and musicians of Austria. The Emperor Franz Josef invited him to call.

Jean Clemens remarked: "Why, Papa, if it keeps on like this, pretty soon there won't be anybody for you to get acquainted with but God." Though Jean meant it innocently enough, it is unfortunately a qualified compliment.

To these years in Vienna belongs Mark Twain's greatest short story, "The Man That Corrupted Hadleyburg," published in *Harper's Magazine* in December, 1899. In this sardonic tale, Mark Twain uncovers the evil lurking under the surface of self-righteous honesty. He had discovered, even in himself, what the underworld calls larceny of the heart. This is the great temptation to get rich quick without honest effort. It is the cowardly motive that drives people to patronize fortune-tellers and to fall for swindlers.

Mark Twain visited soothsayers and palmists. As if afraid to meet life as it came, he wanted to know what might lie ahead, and prepare for it. Strangely enough, one of these charlatans told him he had no sense of humor, and another confused him with his brother Orion. But he seems to have believed them.

Perhaps because of the impression the primitive Negroes had made on him when he was a child, he also had several superstitions. He was alarmed if he got out of bed on the wrong side; he was careful to "touch wood"; he would leave something behind after staying at a place he liked, so that he would be sure to return; he dreaded to have a black cat cross his path. He took seriously mysticism, extrasensory perception, faith healing, and other nonrealistic explanations of phenomena.

Mark's wildly imprudent investments in impractical, even nonsensical, schemes show him as basically the hick in the big city, the easy mark of the confidence man and the swindler. He had been a poor boy, envious of the advantages and the distinctions of the rich. Because he was physically lazy, probably as a result of his early frailness, he hated anything that did not come easily. He was jealous of his associates in Nook Farm because most of them had inherited their basic wealth, not earned it. The somewhat cynical ending of *Tom Sawyer* shows his belief that easy money gains one respect sooner than character alone.

The scene of "The Man That Corrupted Hadleyburg" is again Hannibal. The symbol of the mysterious stranger once more appears. Mark is now a stranger to the people of his home village, who are smug because they are narrowly provincial. He, on the other hand, has seen the world and learned what it has to teach him of man's cowardice and cruelty, indecency and indignity. As a stranger, he plays a trick on the villagers that exposes their self-righteousness as a mask for their larceny of the heart. This is his revenge for their having inflicted on him their strict morality and their stern Calvinism. He now could see through the painted transparency which had made Hannibal appear idyllic. Like Eseldorf, it might have been a paradise for boys, but it was a hell for men. Only the corrupt, Mark Twain implies, can be corrupted; only the falsely moral can be tempted.

Mark Twain had come a long way from his first real story, "The Jumping Frog." Now he had learned enough of life to be able to pass judgment on it with the wry humor of the philosopher. The symbols and the signposts at last were clear.

By January, 1898, he had paid off all the debts occasioned by the failure of the publishing firm less than four years before. When the press of the world got the news, Mark Twain was hailed as a hero.

The achievement was due to Mark's own determination, and the money had come from his copyrights. Credit for the management of it goes to Henry Rogers, who now proceeded to invest Mark's funds and build another fortune for him. Mark, though, was by no means cured of his Colonel Sellers dream of quick and large returns from impractical projects.

Less than a month after he was clear of debt, he was urging Rogers to help him capitalize a company on the basis of his chance to buy the American rights to a carpet-making machine for $1,500,000. Rogers refused to let him sink a penny into the scheme. Shortly thereafter, without consulting Rogers, Mark put $25,000 into a newly invented diet food, "plasmon." He eventually realized $100 on the speculation. It was not Mark Twain's extravagance that had ruined him; it was his investments.

In spite of Mark's new freedom from financial worries, he and his family continued to live in Europe. Not until October, 1900, did he yield to the continuous invitations to return to America. Then he got a resounding welcome.

After nine years of wandering he was glad to be home again. To a reporter who had come out to the *Minnehaha* to interview him before he landed, Mark Twain said: "If I ever get ashore, I am going to break both of my legs so I can't get away again."

The family had decided not to go back to Hartford. Memories of Susy were still too strong for them to be able to enjoy the house where they had all lived together. Instead, Mark rented a house at 14 West Tenth Street in New York City. Later they moved to Riverdale.

He plunged into activities connected with the politics of the time, speaking and writing against the corruption of the Tammany Hall government of New York City. When its candidate for mayor was defeated, Mark facetiously claimed the credit in a jingle he wrote on the fall of the Tammany boss, Richard Croker:

Who killed Croker?
I, said Mark Twain.
I killed the Croker,
I, the Jolly Joker.

He attacked American imperialism in the Philippines just as he had sided with the South Africans against the English and the Boers—all out of general sympathy with the underdog, regardless of economic considerations or the demands of international competition. He made great fun of the pieties of predatory millionaires like John D. Rockefeller, and John Wanamaker. He lobbied vigorously for international copyright protection for all artists.

Every institution in New York invited him to speak at some occasion organized in his honor. Yale University added to the recognition it had given him in 1888 with an honorary Master of Arts degree, by now conferring upon him its Doctor of Letters degree. The University of Missouri made him a Doctor of Law in the following year.

That degree itself seemed to mean less to him than the chance it gave him to revisit his boyhood friends and the scenes of his childhood when he went to Columbia, Missouri, to receive it.

Horace Bixby and others of Mark's surviving riverboat friends met him in St. Louis. "I have become an old man," Mark said to Bixby. "You are still thirty-five."

In Hannibal he saw Laura Hawkins and John Briggs. Briggs and he walked together among the landmarks of their youth, from which Mark Twain had mined the richest of his materials. Mark recalled that he and Briggs had been like brothers once, and he felt they still were.

"Good-bye, John," he said as they parted. "I'll try to meet you—somewhere."

He had kept a faith in an afterlife. Now that faith was stronger.

During those busy first two years after his return to America, Mark Twain wrote only occasional pieces that are of small literary importance. During the summer of 1901, which he spent in the Adirondacks, he produced a burlesque of the Sherlock Holmes stories, *A Double-*

Barreled Detective Story. It is memorable only because of one paragraph in which Mark satirized the rhapsodic bathos of popular nature writing by combining impossible aspects of nature and picturing an oesophagus as a bird. Most of his readers fell for the hoax and still are taken in by it.

"Was It Heaven? or Hell?," written the following summer, was to have a bitterly ironic fulfillment in Mark Twain's own life. In this sentimental story, two women spare their dying sister's feelings by refusing to say that her daughter has died of the disease she caught from her mother. Later that same summer Livy was prostrated with heart disease. She had to be kept quiet and undisturbed. The following winter, Jean contracted pneumonia and almost died. Clara and Mark were hard put to invent lies that would fool the intelligent Livy about Jean's health.

When, in the fall of 1903, Livy had recovered sufficiently to be moved, Mark took her to convalesce in Florence. Fear that he might soon lose her turned Mark Twain's thoughts again to the betrayal of character by greed for worldly things. He wrote another sardonic story, "The $30,000 Bequest," about the destruction of happiness by greed. In his anguish Mark Twain could think of "the damned human race" only as contemptible beings, inferior on the whole to the cats he loved.

Livy lingered through the winter and into the next spring. Then, on June 5, 1904, she died. Mark was brokenhearted. "I am tired and old," he wrote to William Dean Howells. "I wish I were with Livy."

The man who had once loved life so warmly now found it absurd. His mother, Orion and his wife, Susy and Livy, and many of his friends were dead. That September, Pamela died. Jean had been an epileptic for over ten years. Clara suffered a nervous breakdown in the winter of 1904 and had to spend some time in a sanitarium. "The joy of life," Mark Twain wrote, "is turned to aching grief. . . . Death is the only unpoisoned gift earth ever had for [men]."

Yet he could see death's irony, and joke about it. "Each person," he wrote, "is born to one possession which outvalues all his others—his last breath." Adam was "the first great benefactor of our race. He brought death into the world." "All people have ill luck, but Jairus' daughter and Lazarus had the worst."

These epigrams show a perhaps intentional failure to distinguish between the death of the spirit, which can occur while life goes on, and the extinguishing of life itself. He faced that inevitable eventuality bravely. When his friend the actor Sir Henry Irving died in 1905, Mark Twain wrote: "It is a little reminder. My section of the procession has but a little way to go. I could not be sorry if I tried."

On the "little way he had to go" his sense of humor still sustained him. Humor, he said, must be one of the chief attributes of God, mankind's greatest blessing.

He had taken a large house on the southeast corner of Ninth Street and Fifth Avenue in New York, and had moved into it the contents of the Hartford house, which he had sold. It had a billiard room, and there he would sometimes play his favorite game all night long, inventing variations, swearing at a run of bad luck, always contriving to win. Or he would listen to his orchestrelle, a huge, unwieldy mechanical piano-organ which he had transported whenever he went away for the summer. He had learned to like music of a higher quality than that he enjoyed when he was young. Beethoven's *Fifth Symphony* was his favorite.

Mark Twain's mop of hair and his bushy moustache had turned a glistening white, which was accentuated by his ruddy complexion. He took great care of his hair, regarding it as a trademark. Always a flamboyant dresser—he once startled strangers by appearing in a sealskin coat with the fur outside, then very unconventional—he now determined to wear only white, and ordered fourteen white serge suits from his tailor. Even in his old age he never lost his showmanship or his passion for dramatizing himself.

When Mark Twain's seventieth birthday was due, his friends offered to get up a banquet in honor of it. Mark protested that a simple evening with beer and sandwiches would please him more, but no one thought that adequate for America's most celebrated man of letters. The guests at the dinner his friends arranged at Delmonico's included nearly two hundred of the country's leading writers, eager to pay tribute to the man himself as well as to the American spirit he represented.

After they had spoken, Mark Twain arose to address them. "I have achieved my seventy years," he said, "in the usual way: by sticking strictly to a scheme of life which would kill anybody else." Then he detailed his habits of eating "things which didn't agree with me until one or the other of us got the best of it" and of smoking: "I have made it a rule never to smoke more than one cigar at a time."

Finally, he said: "Your invitation honors me, and pleases me because you still keep me in your remembrance, but I am seventy; seventy, and would nestle in the chimney corner, and smoke my pipe, and read my book, and take my rest, wishing you well in all affection, and that when you in your turn shall arrive at pier Number Seventy you may step aboard your waiting ship with a reconciled spirit, and lay your course toward the sinking sun with a contented heart."

Several years earlier, a clerical error in sending Mark

Twain's bills at The Players to Mark himself, instead of to his business manager in Hartford, F. G. Whitmore, had caused Mark to become ill-tempered and arbitrary. He would not forward the bills to Whitmore, and he would not pay them himself. He was expelled from The Players for delinquency in the matter. A group of members vigorously protested this disciplinary action on the part of the club's board of directors, and pleaded with Mark to forget the incident and return to The Players. But he refused to stand for reelection by what he called "that idiot asylum" of a board. The directors then made him an honorary member for life and, as he said, he was "glad to resume business at the old stand."

On January 6, 1906, the eighteenth anniversary of the founders' luncheon at Delmonico's, twenty-two of Mark's friends at The Players organized a dinner to welcome him back to the club. It was then that Albert Bigelow Paine, a fellow Player, persuaded him to write his autobiography. Four days later, Mark began dictating it to a stenographer, with Paine to help him. But Mark Twain stipulated that it was not to be published until long after his death. It was to be a voice from the grave. "On these terms only," Mark Twain wrote, "can a man be approximately frank. He cannot be straightly and unqualifiedly frank either in the grave or out of it." Nevertheless, he allowed some chapters of the *Autobiography* to be published in the *North American Review* before he died.

The *Autobiography* is as full of humor, wit, and charm as everything else Mark Twain wrote that involves and expresses his own personality. It comes closest in style to what he was like as an informal talker, and it indicates the spell he was able to weave around an audience when he lectured. He regarded the text as a communication as private as a love letter, and did not hesitate to denounce or commend people and things he detested or admired as if he were estimating them to an intimate friend. It is, however, an inaccurate record of events and dates, and is often so inconsistent with the facts regarding incidents, relationships, opinions, and business transactions that it is more of an autobiographical novel than a piece of history. But it is the kind of fiction that is more revealing than truth.

Albert Bigelow Paine became Mark Twain's close friend and almost constant companion in the last four years of Mark's life. Mark appointed Paine his literary executor. In that capacity, Paine edited and published many of Mark Twain's papers and letters, thus greatly adding to the future's understanding of the author. He also published a four-volume biography of Mark Twain, an extremely complete record of his life, unfortunately marred by Paine's own prudishness and by having apparently been written in a kneeling position before Paine's private shrine of St. Mark.

Mark Twain had hoped his wanderings were over, but when Oxford University offered him an honorary degree in the spring of 1907, he wrote: "That is a prize which I would go far to get at any time."

When he arrived in England, even the stevedores on the dock cheered him. The King received him. *Punch* dedicated its cover and a front-page cartoon to him, and entertained him at luncheon—the first foreigner in fifty years to be so honored. All England welcomed him as an ambassador of goodwill whose humor had helped break down barriers among peoples, destroy prejudices, and consolidate nations. His degree of Doctor of Letters was conferred on June 30, 1907, with the citation, originally given in Latin: "You shake the sides of the whole world with your merriment."

When he returned to America, Mark Twain pulled out from among his unpublished manuscripts one that he had conceived nearly forty years before after hearing Captain Ned Wakeman's account of a dream in which he had visited heaven. Mark had begun the story as a parody of *The Gates Ajar,* an 1868 novel of sickening sentimentality, by Elizabeth Ward, which was popular in the return-to-religion craze of the post-Civil War years. That was not a good time in which to publish it. But Mark had not forgotten the breezy captain of the *America;* he had appeared as Captain Hurricane Jones in Mark Twain's "Some Rambling Notes of an Idle Excursion" in 1877.

Since 1868, attitudes toward heaven and hell had changed, and these localities were being thought of less as literal places than as states of mind. Mark Twain modernized the story, which *Harper's Magazine* accepted for its December, 1908, and January, 1909, issues, and later published as a book. The story expresses Mark Twain's views on the insignificance of man, despite his self-importance, and the minuteness of earth in relation to the other worlds of the universe. It is another sermon against smugness and provinciality, but this time it is delivered with much of the old Mark Twain humor. The heavenly choir strikes up an anthem, for example, and Captain Stormfield reports that "it was noble music, but the uneducated chipped in and spoilt it, just as the congregations used to do on earth."

Mark had found the pressures of city life tiring. In 1906 he had bought some two hundred acres of land near Paine's summer home in Redding, Connecticut. The $30,000 he had got from the sale of the serial rights to his *Autobiography* he turned over to John Mead Howells, the architect son of his old friend and editor, saying that he did not want to see the house he commissioned "until the cat is purring on the hearth." Now, on June 28, 1908, he moved into the handsome Italian villa Howells had built for him on a hilltop. Mark named the place "Stormfield," for part of it had been paid for by the proceeds from his last book.

The following year, Clara was married there to Ossip Gabrilowitsch, the pianist, whom she had met several years before in Vienna when she was studying piano with Theodor Leschetizky. Joseph Twichell performed the ceremony, and Mark Twain wore his scarlet and gray Oxford gown. That Christmas Eve, Jean was found dead in her bathtub after an epileptic seizure.

The death of his youngest daughter filled Mark Twain's cup of sorrow to overflowing. He had been suffering from bronchitis and from angina pectoris. The only effort he made to get well was to spend the winter in Bermuda, where he played miniature golf with Woodrow Wilson, and also found companionship in young Helen Allen, with whose parents he was staying.

By the end of March, 1910, Mark's pains were so intense and frequent that the Allens advised Paine to come to Bermuda and take him home to Stormfield. By the time they got there, Mark could talk very little, and read less, and his mind seemed to dwell on the problems of identity which always puzzled him. One of these was the problem of dual personality. He made references to its occurrences in history and in literature, and particularly to Robert Louis Stevenson's Dr. Jekyll and Mr. Hyde. Possibly he was making one last effort to reconcile Samuel Langhorne Clemens and Mark Twain.

On the night of April 20, Halley's Comet blazed in the sky. Early the next evening Mark Twain died.

Dressed in his favorite white, he was taken on his final trip to New York. Thousands came to pay their last respects to him in the Brick Church, then on Fifth Avenue. William Dean Howells came, too. "I knew them all," he said, "sages, poets, peers, critics, humorists, but Clemens was sole, incomparable, the Lincoln of our literature."

CHRONOLOGY

1835 Samuel Langhorne Clemens born, Florida, Missouri, November 30.

1839 Clemens family moves to Hannibal, Missouri, November.

1847 John Marshall Clemens dies, March 24.

1848 Samuel Clemens begins apprenticeship as a typesetter on the Hannibal *Gazette*, later becoming assistant editor on that newspaper and on the *Hannibal Daily Journal*.

1852 First appearance in print beyond Hannibal: "The Dandy Frightening the Squatter" in *The Carpet-Bag*, May 1.

1853 Leaves Hannibal to begin his wanderings.

1855 Joins his brother Orion in his printing shop in Keokuk, Iowa.

1857 Begins apprenticeship as a Mississippi River steamboat pilot.

1861 Leaves piloting due to outbreak of Civil War. Brief soldiering experience. Goes to Nevada with Orion, arriving August 14.

1862 Joins staff of *Territorial Enterprise*, Virginia City, Nevada, August.

1863 Adopts pen name of Mark Twain, February 2.

1864 Leaves Virginia City for San Francisco, California, May 28.

1865 "The Jumping Frog" published in the *Saturday Press*, New York, November 18.

1866 Trip to Sandwich Islands (Hawaii), March. *Hornet* scoop, July 19. First public lecture, San Francisco, October 2.

1867 Sails on *Quaker City* for Europe and the Holy Land, June 8. Meets Olivia Langdon, December 23.

1869 *The Innocents Abroad* published, July 20.

1870 Marries Olivia Langdon, February 2. Settles in Buffalo, New York.

1871 Moves to Nook Farm, Hartford, Connecticut, in autumn.

1872 *Roughing It* published, February.

1873 *The Gilded Age* published, December.

1876 *The Adventures of Tom Sawyer* published, December.

1877 Whittier Birthday speech, December 17.

1880 *A Tramp Abroad* published, March 13.

1881 *The Prince and the Pauper* published, December.

1884 *The Adventures of Huckleberry Finn* published, December. Charles L. Webster and Company established.

1885 Begins investing in Paige typesetter. *Memoirs of General Grant* published by Charles L. Webster and Company.

1889 *A Connecticut Yankee in King Arthur's Court* published, December.

1891 Begins nine years' "exile" in Europe, June 6.

1894 Charles L. Webster and Company fails, April 18. *Pudd'nhead Wilson* published, November.

1895 *Joan of Arc* serialized, April to December. (Published in book form, May, 1896.) Lecture tour around the world begun July 14, ending July 31, 1896.

1896 Susy Clemens dies, August 18.

1897 *Following the Equator* published, November.

1898 Emerges from bankruptcy, January.

1900 Returns to America, October 15.

1904 Olivia Clemens dies, June 5.

1906 Begins *Autobiography,* published posthumously.

1907 Receives honorary degree of Doctor of Literature from Oxford University, June 26.

1910 Mark Twain dies, April 21.

BIBLIOGRAPHY

Virtually all the works Mark Twain approved for publication during his lifetime are contained in the thirty-seven volumes of *The Writings of Mark Twain,* published from 1907 to 1918 (New York and London: Gabriel Wells). The "Stormfield Edition" (New York and London: Harper & Brothers, 1929) was printed from the same plates and includes the Paine biography.

Since then, the literary executors of the Mark Twain estate, and editors Albert Bigelow Paine, Bernard De Voto, Dixon Wecter, and Henry Nash Smith, have edited or authorized for publication much material, both literary and autobiographical, found among Mark Twain's papers after his death. The most important are the following:

Mark Twain in Eruption, edited by Bernard De Voto. New York: Harper & Brothers, 1940.

Report from Paradise, edited by Dixon Wecter. New York: Harper & Brothers, 1952.

The Autobiography of Mark Twain, edited by Charles Neider. New York: Harper & Brothers, 1959.

Letters from the Earth, edited by Bernard De Voto. New York: Harper & Brothers, 1962.

The Forgotten Writings of Mark Twain, edited by Henry Duskis. New York: Citadel Press, 1963.

BIBLIOGRAPHY

Out of the mass of biographical and critical works on Mark Twain, the author of this book is most indebted to the following:

Allen, Jerry. *The Adventures of Mark Twain.* Boston: Little, Brown and Company, 1954.

Andrews, Kenneth R. *Nook Farm—Mark Twain's Hartford Circle.* Cambridge: Harvard University Press, 1950.

Bellamy, Gladys Carmen. *Mark Twain as a Literary Artist.* Norman: University of Oklahoma Press, 1950.

Brashear, Minnie M. *Mark Twain, Son of Missouri.* New York: Russell & Russell, Inc., 1964.

Clemens, Clara. *My Father, Mark Twain.* New York & London: Harper & Brothers, 1931.

De Voto, Bernard. *Mark Twain's America.* Boston: Little, Brown and Company, 1932.

———. *Mark Twain at Work.* Cambridge: Harvard University Press, 1942.

Ferguson, DeLancey. *Mark Twain: Man and Legend.* Indianapolis: The Bobbs-Merrill Co., 1943.

Lawton, Mary. *A Lifetime with Mark Twain: The Memories of Katy Leary, His Faithful Friend and Servant.* New York: Harcourt, Brace & Co., 1925.

Mack, Effie M. *Mark Twain in Nevada.* New York: Charles Scribner's Sons, 1947.

Meltzer, Milton (ed.). *Mark Twain Himself.* New York: Thomas Y. Crowell Company, 1960.

Paine, Albert Bigelow. *Mark Twain, a Biography.* New York: Harper & Brothers, 1912.

Wagenknecht, Edward. *Mark Twain: the Man and His Work* (rev. ed.). Norman: University of Oklahoma Press, 1961.

Webster, Samuel C. *Mark Twain, Business Man.* Boston: Little, Brown and Company, 1946.

Wecter, Dixon. *Sam Clemens of Hannibal.* Boston: Houghton Mifflin Company, 1952.

INDEX

INDEX